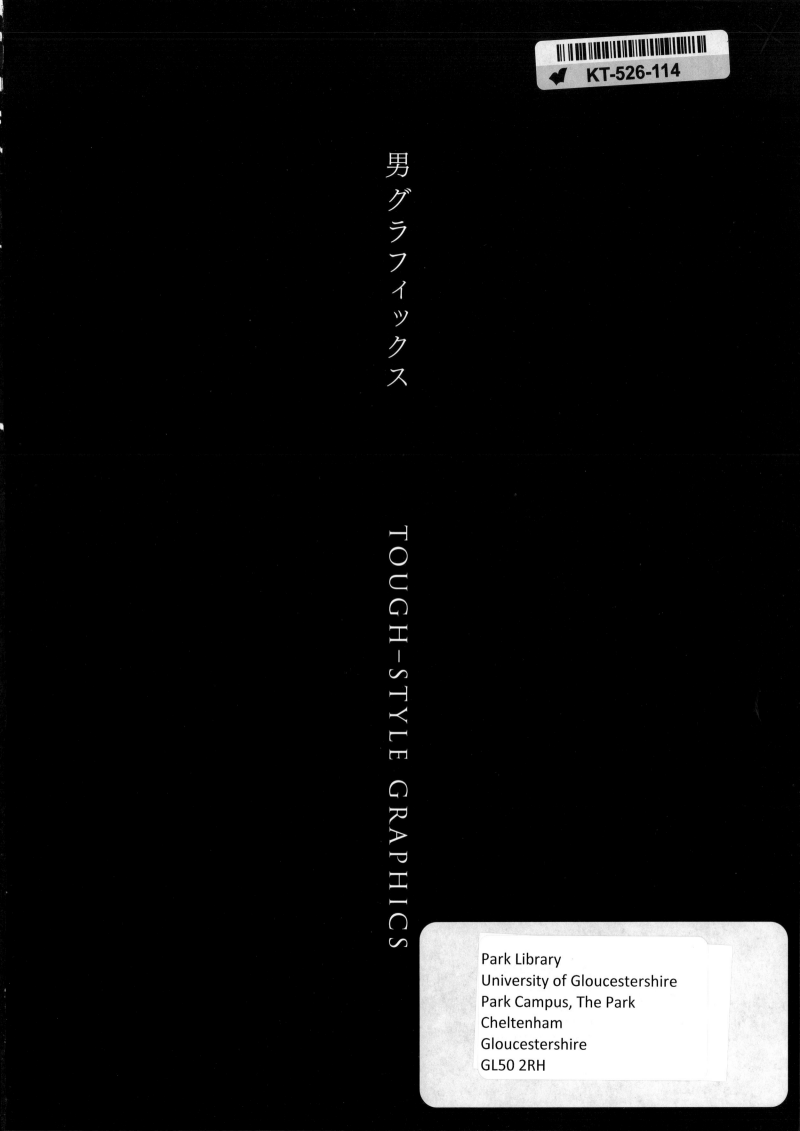

男 グラフィックス

TOUGH-STYLE GRAPHICS

TOUGH-STYLE GRAPHICS

PIE BOOKS
2-32-4, Minami-Otsuka, Toshima-ku, Tokyo 170-0005 JAPAN
Tel : +81-3-5395-4811 Fax : +81-3-5395-4812

e-mail :
editor@piebooks.com
sales@piebooks.com
http://www.piebooks.com

ISBN978-4-89444-678-6 C3070
Printed in Japan

UNIVERSITY OF
GLOUCESTERSHIRE
at Cheltenham and Gloucester

Park Library
University of Gloucestershire
Park Campus, The Park, Cheltenham,
Gloucestershire GL50 2RH

CONTENTS

TOUGH
009 - 062

ACTIVE
063 - 108

CHIC
109 - 142

AVANT-GARDE
143 - 192

FOREWORD

強くて伝わる「男」

なデザイン

「男グラフィックス」という本書のタイトルに、驚かれた方も多いと思います。

本書タイトルの「男」は名詞ではなく、形容詞としての「男」。

力強く、切れがよく、潔い。

本書では「男」をこのように定義し、近年目立ち始めたエッジの効いたデザインにフォーカスします。

なぜ、今「男」なのか。

膨大な情報があふれた現代では、狙ったターゲットにメッセージを届ける「伝達力の高い」デザインが求められています。

そのため、情報や色をそぎ落とし、強い印象に仕上げたデザインが求められています。

また、男性の購買意欲が増し、男性向けのマーケットが広がっていることも、「男」なデザインが増えた要因の一つではないでしょうか。

本書では広告、プロダクト、ショップイメージ、企業アイデンティティなど、さまざまな分野の「男」なデザインを紹介していきます。

男を感じさせるデザインの中にもより力強いもの、カジュアルなものなど、さまざまなバリエーションが存在します。

そこで弊書では、「TOUGH/タフ」「ACTIVE/アクティブ」「CHIC/シック」「AVANT-GARDEアヴァンギャルド」の4つのテイスト別に作品を紹介させていただきました。

各カテゴリーの扉には「男」なデザインを手がけていらっしゃる代表的なデザイナーの方々にデザインに関すること、そして有彩色ではないにもかかわらず、もっとも強い印象を残す色である「黒」という色の扱い方についてのインタビューを掲載しています。

みなさまにデザインについてお考えいただける一助になれば幸いです。

最後に本書の制作にご協力いただきました

「男」なデザイナーのみなさまに心からお礼を申し上げます。

ピエブックス編集部

FOREWORD

Powerful and cool

introducing "tough

style" graphics.

Powerful, razor-sharp and fearless.

In this book, we focus on the edgy design style known as "tough style" that has risen to prominence in recent years and introduce various examples of tough-style design from fields such as advertising, products, corporate identity and store branding.

Tough style. Why now?

In a world in the midst of an information explosion, marketers need design styles that hit their target. Tough style reduces the visual and textual information to a minimum, thereby producing a powerful impact.

More companies today also want universal branding for their worldwide endeavors. The quest for design styles that work on anyone regardless of gender or nationality and the expanding male market with an increasing appetite for consumption may be one of the reasons the number of "tough" design styles is on the increase.

Tough design styles range in scope from ultra-powerful to casual. To best show their variety, we've grouped the works presented herein under the four loose categories of Tough, Active, Chic, and Avant-garde.

On the cover pages of these categories we feature interviews with top designers active in the field of tough design discussing their approaches to design and the use of the "achromatic color" black.

The look of the new design is robust and penetrating and should provide not only graphic designers but also designers working in other areas with lots of new, fresh ideas. We hope it will aid designers in thinking about all forms of design.

And last but not least, our heartfelt thanks goes to those wonderful "tough" designers who were involved in the production of this book.

Pie Books Editorial Department

EDITORIAL NOTES

A アイテム名 Items

B クライアント ［業種名］ Client ［Type of Industry］

C スタッフクレジット
ECD：エグゼクティブ・クリエイティブ・ディレクター Executive Creative Director
SCD：シニア・クリエイティブ・ディレクター Senior Creative Director
CD：クリエイティブ・ディレクター Creative Director
AD：アート・ディレクター Art Director
D：デザイナー Designer
I：イラストレーター Illustrator
CW：コピーライター Copywriter
P：フォトグラファー Photographer
DF：制作会社 Design Firm
SB：作品提供社 Submittor

D カテゴリー Category

※上記以外の制作者呼称は省略せずに掲載しています。
All other production titles are unabbreviated.

※本書に掲載されている店名、店舗写真、販促ツール、商品などは、すべて２００８年３月時点での情報になります。
All in store-related information, including shop name, photography, promotional items and products are accurate as of March 2008.

※本書に掲載されているキャンペーン、プロモーションは、既に終了しているものもありますので、ご了承ください。
Please note that some campaigns and promotions are no longer deployed.

※作品提供者の意向によりデータの一部を記載していない場合があります。
Please note that some credit information has been omitted at the request of the submittor.

※各企業に附随する、"株式会社、（株）" および "有限会社、（有）" は表記を省略させて頂きました。
The "kabushiki gaisha (K.K.)" and "yugen gaisha (Ltd.)" portions of all Japanese company name have been omitted.

※本書に記載された企業名・商品名は、掲載各社の商標または登録商標です。
The company and product names that appear in this book are published and/or registered trademarks.

TOUGH

Powerful / Solid / Massive
力強い / 骨太な / 重々しい

Kenjiro Sano — a "tough" designer talks about "tough-style" design

Advertising is about communication. I start by thinking about what kind of look or image I am going to give to the product so as to be able to convey just that, to clarify a vague image. Art directors don't necessarily have to be artistic but they do have to have an ability to express the look or a function of the product in concrete terms. Design is not about ornamentation, it is about creating an "identity" that is easy for anyone to comprehend. I think the easiest way to describe it would be "strong design that communicates a message."

What black embodies

Black is a color that embodies simplicity, clarity and boldness. It has a presence that supports the kind of gutsy design that everyone gets at first glance.

KENJIRO SANO
Art director. Principal of MR_DESIGN
Born 1972 in Tokyo. In 1996, he joined HAKUHODO Inc., and after 12 years with the ad agency and Hakuhodo Design, launched MR_DESIGN in 2008. Among the many honors he has received are the MIURA-JUN Award, the NY ADC Award, ONE SHOW DESIGN,D&AD, the Tokyo TDC Prize, the Tokyo ADC Award, the JAGDA New Designer Award. Some poster entered in the permanent collection of Die Neue Sammlung (Munich) in 2008. www.mr-design.jp

His Works / P13, P50-51, P53, P95, P168, P173, P177

「男」なデザイナーの語る「男」なデザイン／佐野研二郎

デザインはコミュニケーションを円滑にする行為。現在メディアも広がりみんな忙しいから複雑な構造なものを理解する時間がない。すぐに伝わるスピードの早いコミュニケーションでなければ効かなくなっています。そのような時代に届く表現へと仕上げるために、まず商品やサービスを「どのような人格、佇まいにすれば適切に伝わるのか」という点から考え、曖昧な要素を排除、圧縮していきます。デザインは装飾ではなく「人格」を作ること。分かりやすい、誰にでも通じる。そんな簡単に言語化できる表現が「強くて、伝わる」デザインだと思います。

黒が具現化するもの

黒は「SIMPLE, CLEAR, BOLD」を具現化できる色。かんたんで太くて、ハッキリしている。誰もが一瞬で分かる骨太なデザインを支えてくれる存在です。

佐野研二郎
アートディレクター／クリエイティブディレクター MR_DESIGN 代表。
1972年東京生まれ。博報堂、HAKUHODO DESIGNを経て2008年にMR_DESIGNを設立。国内外で商品開発やシンボルマーク、キャラクターデザインをはじめとして広告デザイン、店頭POPまでトータルなアートディレクションを行う。受賞にみうらじゅん賞、ニューヨークADC賞、ONE SHOW DESIGN、D&AD、東京ADC賞、東京TDC賞、JAGDA新人賞など。2008年ノイエ・ザムルング（ミュンヘン）にポスター数点がパーマネントコレクションされる。www.mr-design.jp

作品掲載ページ／P13, P50-51, P53, P95, P168, P173, P177

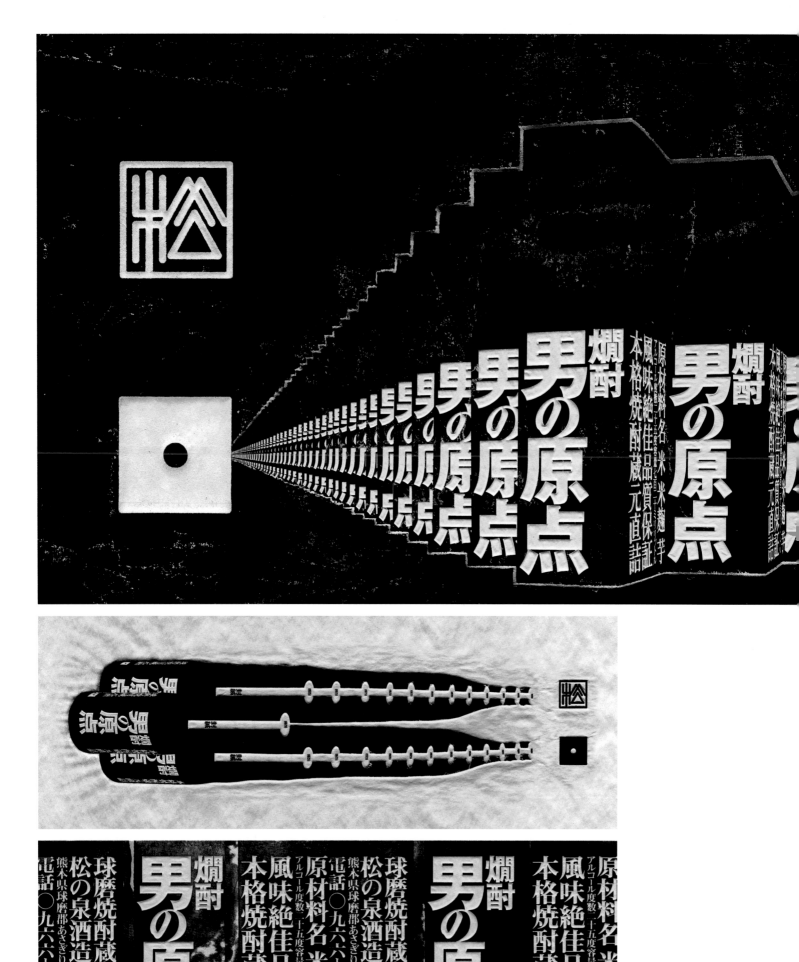

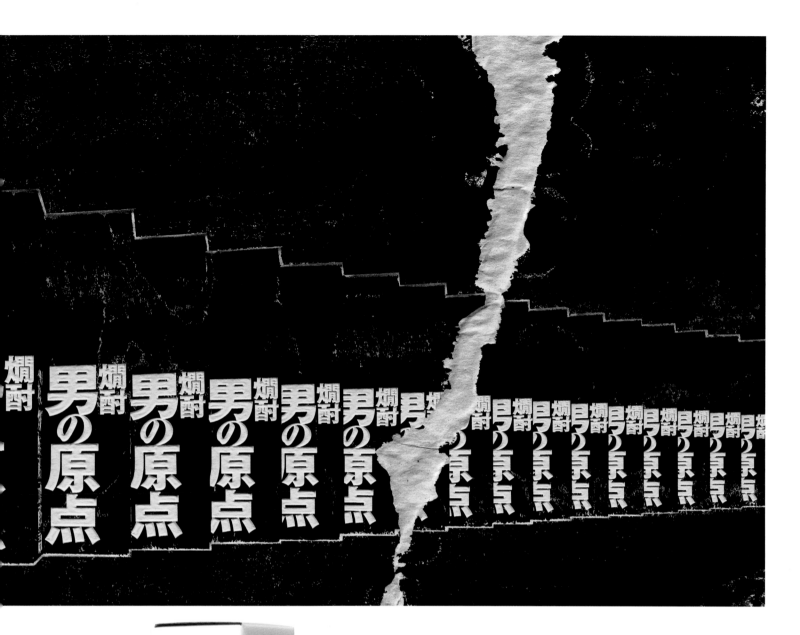

商品案内ポスター、パッケージ /
PRODUCT PROMOTION POSTER, PACKAGE

東レ［総合化学製品メーカー］
Toray Industries,Inc.［General chemical products manufacturer］
CD, AD, D: 小磯裕司　Yuji Koiso
SB: 日本デザインセンター　NIPPON DESIGN CENTER,INC.

商品案内DM / PRODUCT PROMOTION DM

アトウ ［アパレル］
ato ［Apparel］
AD, D, SB: 米津智之　Tomoyuki Yonezu
P: 土井浩一郎 (angle)　Koichiro Doi (angle)

商品案内ポスター / PRODUCT PROMOTION POSTER

日産自動車 ［自動車メーカー］
Nissan Motor Co.,Ltd. ［Auto manufactures］
CD: 塚田雅人　Masato Tsukada
AD: 佐野研二郎　Kenjiro Sano
D: 岡本和樹　Kazuki Okamoto／原野賢太郎　Kentaro Harano
P: 瀧本幹也　Mikiya Takimoto／梅沢 勉　Tsutomu Umezawa
CW: 田中量司　Ryoji Tanaka
SB, DF: 博報堂　HAKUHODO Inc.／MR_DESIGN　MR_DESIGN

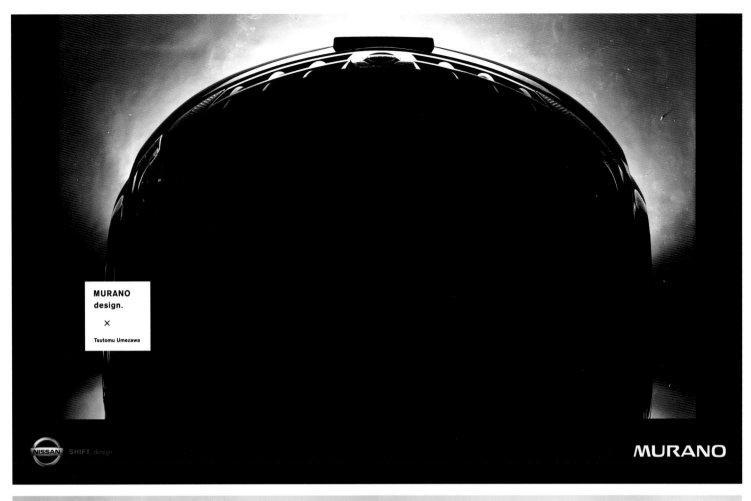

MURANO
design.

×

Tsutomu Umezawa

NISSAN SHIFT_design

MURANO

MURANO
design.

×

Mikiya Takimoto

SHIFT_design

MURANO

そのファンは、何百万回も回った後、
さらに使いまわせる。

部品の寿命は、製品の寿命より長い。私たちは再使用を徹底し、CO_2の
排出量を削減するため、あらかじめ解体しやすいように設計された部品
を採用しています。空冷ファンには、工具を必要とせず、より素早く簡単
な取り外しを可能にする「スナップフィット組み立て方式」を導入。部
品を傷つけない丁寧な分別を実現することで、リユース率の大幅な向上
に成功しました。リユース部品を使用した複写機・複合機の生産台数
はすでに、延べ29万台を突破。機器の熱だけでなく、地球温暖化の熱
も冷ます部品がある。富士ゼロックスは、新品同等の品質を保証した
リユース部品で、資源循環のサイクルもまわしつづけていきます。

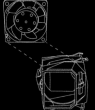

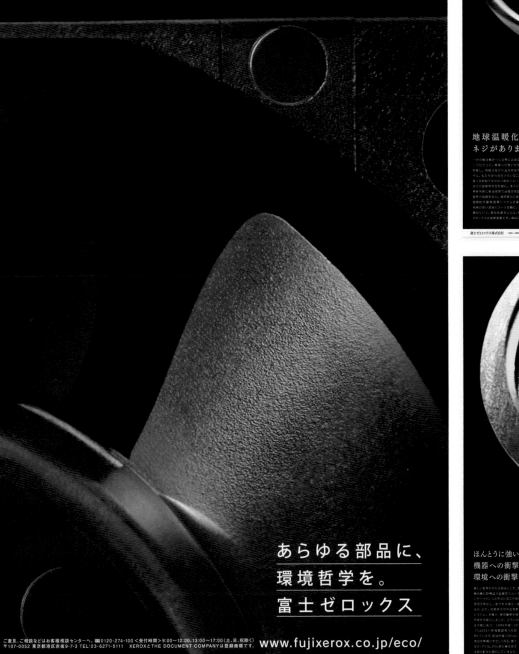

あらゆる部品に、
環境哲学を。
富士ゼロックス

www.fujixerox.co.jp/eco/

地球温暖化をとめる
ネジがあります。

あらゆる部品に、
環境哲学を。
富士ゼロックス

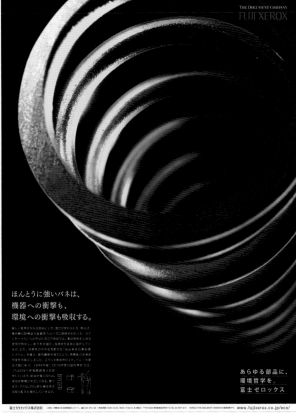

ほんとうに強いバネは、
機器への衝撃も、
環境への衝撃も吸収する。

あらゆる部品に、
環境哲学を。
富士ゼロックス

企業ブランド新聞広告、雑誌広告 ／
COMPANY BRANDING NEWSPAPER AD, MAGAZINE AD

富士ゼロックス ［電子機器製造・販売］
Fuji Xerox Co.,Ltd. [Electric manufacture & Sales]
CD: 福島和人　Kazuto Fukushima
AD: 平野光太郎　Kotaro Hirano
D: 高嶋紀男　Norio Takashima / 清水千春　Chiharu Shimizu
P: 高橋秀行　Hideyuki Takahashi / 西田宗之　Muneyuki Nishida
CW: 横山慶太　Keita Yokoyama
DF: サラッド　salad Inc.
SB: 博報堂　HAKUHODO INC.

商品案内リーフレット /
PRODUCT PROMOTION LEAFLET

アライズ ［タイヤの販売会社］
ALLIES ［Tire selling agent］
AD, D: 栗原幸治　Koji Kurihara
P: 田中康裕　Yasuhiro Tanaka
CW: 伊藤慎　Makoto Ito
DF, SB: クリ・ラボ　KURI-LAB.

O:SA'KA" 2007   O:SA'KA" 2007   O:SA'KA" 2007   O:SA'KA" 2007
100M   200M   400M   800M   1500M   5000M
10000M   20KM RACE WALK   50KM RACE WALK
MARATHON   3000M STEEPLECHASE   100M
HURDLES   110M HURDLES   400M HURDLES
4X100M RELAY   4X400M RELAY   HIGH JUMP
POLE VAULT   LONG JUMP   TRIPLE JUMP
SHOT PUT   DISCUS THROW   HAMMER THROW
JAVELIN THROW   DECATHLON   HEPTATHLON
O:SA'KA" 2007   O:SA'KA" 2007   O:SA'KA" 2007   O:SA'KA" 2007

O:SA'KA" 2007   O:SA'KA" 2007   O:SA'KA" 2007   O:SA'KA" 2007
100M   200M   400M   800M   1500M   5000M
10000M   20KM RACE WALK   50KM RACE WALK
MARATHON   3000M STEEPLECHASE   100M
HURDLES   110M HURDLES   400M HURDLES
4X100M RELAY   4X400M RELAY   HIGH JUMP
POLE VAULT   LONG JUMP   TRIPLE JUMP
SHOT PUT   DISCUS THROW   HAMMER THROW
JAVELIN THROW   DECATHLON   HEPTATHLON
O:SA'KA" 2007   O:SA'KA" 2007   O:SA'KA" 2007   O:SA'KA" 2007

競技大会イベントルック /
SPORT COMPETITON EVENT LOOK

財団法人IAAF世界陸上2007大阪大会組織委員会 ［団体］
ORGANISING Committe for the 11th IAAF World Championships in
Athletics OSAKA 2007 [Association]
CD, AD: 水野 学　Manabu Mizuno
D: 上村 昌　Masaru Uemura
DF, SB: グッドデザインカンパニー　good design company

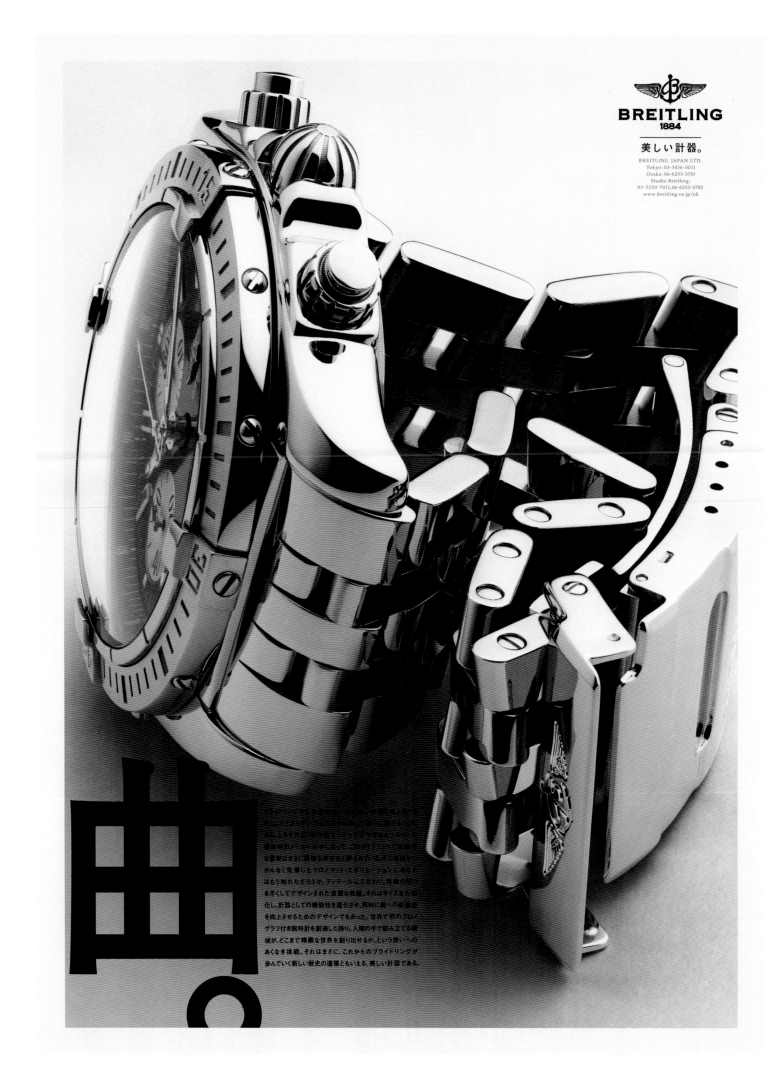

ブランド新聞広告 2005 /
BRANDING NEWSPAPER AD 2005

ブライトリング・ジャパン [時計販売代理店]
BREITLING JAPAN LTD. [Watch selling agent]
CD: 宮田 識　Satoru Miyata
CD, CW: 広瀬正明　Masaaki Hirose
AD, P: 古屋友章　Tomoaki Furuya
D: 平野篤史　Atsushi Hirano
DIGITAL ARTIST: 赤木康隆　Yasutaka Akagi
DF, SB: ドラフト　DRAFT Co.,Ltd.

ブランド新聞広告 2003 /
BRANDING NEWSPAPER AD 2003

ブライトリング・ジャパン [時計販売代理店]
BREITLING JAPAN LTD. [Watch selling agent]
CD, AD: 宮田 識　Satoru Miyata
CD, CW: 広瀬正明　Masaaki Hirose
AD, P: 古屋友章　Tomoaki Furuya
PR: 西面俊秀　Toshihide Nishio
DF, SB: ドラフト　DRAFT Co.,Ltd.

BREITLING

EXHIBITION & PRESENTATION 2006

拝啓 陽春の候 皆様にはますますご清栄のこととお慶び申し上げます。

ここに2006年の展示会＆プレゼンテーションの開催をご案内いたします。ことし私たちは、ブライトリングの

広告のキャッチフレーズとして「奇跡」という言葉を掲げました。それは精緻な究極の複雑さをもつブライトリング

の想像を超える美しさを表現したものです。奇跡とは、あり得ないことです。しかし奇跡を呼ぶという言葉が

あるように、ひとつひとつ小さな努力を積み重ねていくところには、想像もしないことが起き得るのだと思います。

CHRONOMAT EVOLUTION、そしてBREITLING for BENTLEYという新しいジャンルへの挑戦と世界的な成功。

伝統と革新という哲学をもって新しい未来に挑戦しつづける努力こそがブライトリングなのです。今年も、期待を

超える新作の発表、皆様のマーケティング活動を強力にサポートする総合戦略のプレゼンテーション。さらなる情熱を

もって充実したプログラムを展開したいと思います。ぜひご参加くださいますよう心よりお待ち申し上げております。

ブライトリング・ジャパン株式会社

BREITLING EXHIBITION & PRESENTATION 2006

BREITLING

BREITLING JAPAN TOKYO　Shibakoen build. 2-2-22, Shibakoen, Minato-ku, Tokyo 〒105-0011 tel.03-3456-0011 fax.03-3456-0012
BREITLING JAPAN OSAKA　Yodoko no.2 build. 4-2-13, Bakuro-machi, Chuo-ku, Osaka 〒541-0059 tel.06-6253-3701 fax.06-6253-3703

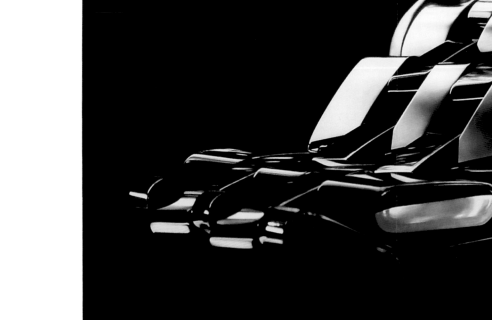

展示会案内状 2006 / EXHIBITION INVITATION 2006

ブライトリング・ジャパン [時計販売代理店]
BREITLING JAPAN LTD. [Watch selling agent]
CD: 宮田 識　Satoru Miyata
CD, CW: 広瀬正明　Masaaki Hirose
AD, P: 古屋友章　Tomoaki Furuya
D: 平野篤史　Atsushi Hirano
P: 小川貴光　Takamitsu Ogawa
DIGITAL ARTIST: 赤木康隆　Yasutaka Akagi
DF, SB: ドラフト　DRAFT Co.,Ltd.

OSAKA 5/18［木］10:00-17:00 19［金］10:00-16:30
※19:00よりメンバーズサロン開催の為、最終入場等が16:00となります。

UMEDA STELLA HALL

大阪府大阪市北区中崎西1・1・88
梅田スカイビル タワーウエスト3F

JR「大阪駅」中央北口より、徒歩で約9分
阪急「梅田駅」茶屋町口より、徒歩で約9分
地下鉄御堂筋線「梅田駅」5番出口より、徒歩で約9分

TOKYO 5/25［木］10:00-17:00 26［金］10:00-16:30
※19:00よりメンバーズサロン開催の為、最終入場等が16:00となります。

EBISU GARDEN HALL

東京都目黒区三田1・15・2
恵比寿ガーデンプレイス内

JR山手線・埼京線「恵比寿駅」東口より
スカイウォークで約5分
地下鉄日比谷線「恵比寿駅」JR方面出口より
スカイウォークで約10分

奇蹟。

奇蹟という言葉を辞書で引くと、常識では考えられない神秘的な出来事、とある。
この美しい曲線で構成された時計をじっと見ていると、まさにその言葉が浮かび上がってくる。
1884年、スイスの小さな村から始まったこの時計の歴史物語には、幾多の人が関わっている。
クロノグラフというストップウォッチ機構を腕時計に搭載しようと考えた人。
リセットボタンや回転式計算尺を考えた人。クォーツの波に押された逆境の時代にも、
ひるむことなく機械式時計の大いなる価値を信じて事業を継承した人。
その情熱を妥協のないカタチにした、ムーブメントをつくる職人。
針や文字盤やケースをつくる職人。信念と揺るぎのない誇りを持ち続けながら
120年という永い時間に関わった人の、その誰が欠けても、その誰の意志が欠けても、
この美しい時計はいまここに存在しないのだ。いうなれば、その存在は奇蹟なのだ。
官能的でもある流麗な曲線。芸術的ともいえるディテールの見事さ。
しかしそれを超えた美しさと魅力を感じる理由は、そこにある。ブライトリング。

BREITLING
1884

021

BREITLING EXHIBITION & PRESENTATION 2007

BREITLING EXHIBITION & PRESENTATION 2007
BREITLING JAPAN TOKYO Shibakoen build, 2-2-22, Shibakoen, Minato-ku, Tokyo, Japan 105-0011 Tel. 03-3436-0011 Fax. 03-3436-0012
BREITLING JAPAN OSAKA Yodoko No.2 build, 4-2-15, Bakuro-machi, Chuo-ku, Osaka, Japan 541-0059 Tel. 06-6253-3701 Fax. 06-6253-3703

展示会案内状 2007 / EXHIBITION INVITATION 2007

ブライトリング・ジャパン [時計販売代理店]
BREITLING JAPAN LTD. [Watch selling agent]
CD: 宮田 識 Satoru Miyata
CD, CW: 広瀬正明 Masaaki Hirose
AD, P: 古屋友章 Tomoaki Furuya
D, P: 平野篤史 Atsushi Hirano
P: 小川貴光 Takamitsu Ogawa
PR: 樋野晶子 Akiko Hino
DF, SB: ドラフト DRAFT Co.,Ltd.

聖域。

入社案内 ／ RECRUITMENT BROCHURE

三菱UFJ信託銀行 ［信託銀行］
Mitsubishi UFJ Trust and Banking Corporation ［Trust bank］
CD, CW: 梅田大輔　Daisuke Umeda
CD: 前畑彰彦　Akihiko Maehata
AD: 小林洋介　Yosuke Kobayashi
D: 坂本尚美　Naomi Sakamoto
P: 黒澤康成　Yasunari Kurosawa
CW: 松本セイヤ　Seiya Matsumoto
PR: 永井美奈子　Minako Nagai
DF, SB: イー　E.Co.,Ltd.

入社案内 ／ RECRUITMENT BROCHURE

三菱UFJ信託銀行 ［信託銀行］
Mitsubishi UFJ Trust and Banking Corporation ［Trust bank］
CD, CW: 梅田大輔　Daisuke Umeda
CD: 松原秀宜　Hidetaka Matsubara
AD: 小林洋介　Yosuke Kobayashi
D: 坂本尚美　Naomi Sakamoto ／ 森茂和美　Kazumi Morimo
P: 友野 正　Tadashi Tomono ／ 宇田幸彦　Yukihiko Uda
CW: 松本セイヤ　Seiya Matsumoto
PR: 永井美奈子　Minako Nagai
DF, SB: イー　E.Co.,Ltd.

Go Ahead With Trustship! vol. 0

TRUST BANKER.

トラストバンカー。それは、全財産をまかせるに足る人のこと。

その旅は、
快適でも安全でもありません。

仕事は旅に似ている。私たちはそう考えます。

旅にも、道先案内人つきの快適な旅と、その先に何があるか見えない危険な旅があります。

人を成長へと導くのは、危ない旅。危機に出くわし、それを切り抜ける。

言葉も考え方も違う人と出会い、ぶつかり合う。

パックツアーでは出会えないエピソードたちが人の幅を大きくする。仕事も同じです。

恵まれた環境で働けば、毎日が幸福で安全です。けれど、タフにはなれない。

あなたが素早く成長したいなら、厳しい世界に自分を置きませんか。

ここには、みずから困難にとびこむ向こう見ずな大人たちがいます。

私たち東京エレクトロンは、半導体の製造装置を作り出すメーカーです。

半導体の世界はめまぐるしく進化し、それを生み出す装置の世界もめまぐるしく進化します。

新しいことをするのは、本当に怖い。だけど、それを乗り越える野心があるからできる。

そして、成功も失敗もすべて自分のせいだと言いきれる。

その厳しさが快感だと社員はいいます。

ところで、あなたはどんな大人になりたいですか。

荒野を歩くように、
仕事をしないか。

成長は、
危険な旅からはじまる。

人材募集雑誌広告 / RECRUTING MAGAZINE AD

東京エレクトロン [半導体製造装置会社]
Tokyo Electron [Semiconductor manufacturer]
CD: 鈴木優輔　Yusuke Suzuki
AD: 小林洋介　Yosuke Kobayashi
D: 新津美香　Mika Niitsu
P: 友野正　Tadashi Tomono
CW: 戸部二美　Fumi Tobe
DIGITAL ARTIST: 千原光一　Koichi Chihara
SB: イー　E.Co.,Ltd.

ゴルフコンペ告知ポスター /
GOLF TOURNAMENT ANNOUNCEMENT POSTER

エンターブレイン [出版社]
ENTERBRAIN INC. [Publisher]
AD, D: 原大輔　Daisuke Hara
DF, SB: スロウ　SLOW inc.

素材が変われば、世界が変わる。

クルマ社会のさらなる進歩に、東洋紡の自動車部材。

企業案内ポスター /
COMPANY PROMOTION POSTER

東洋紡 [製品メーカー]
TOYOBO CO.,LTD. [Manufacture]
CD: 三條場 章 Akira Sanjoba
AD, D: 福森正紀 Masaki Fukumori
P: 森山智彦 Tomohiko Moriyama
CW: 片田英二 Eiji Katada
DF: 博報堂 関西支社 HAKUHODO Inc. Kansai Office
CG: 山岸純 Jun Yamagishi
DF, SB: スリーアンドコー Three & co.

シーズンカタログ / **SEASONAL CATALOG**

アバハウスインターナショナル [アパレル]
ABAHOUSE INTERNATIONAL CO. [Apparel]
AD, D: 野尻大作 Daisaku Nojiri
P: 山本光男 Mitsuo Yamamoto
DF, SB: ground ground

LIQUIDROOM PRESENTS

VITALIC

DJs TAKKYU ISHINO
DJ WADA (CO-FUSION)

2006.11.17 FRIDAY at LIQUIDROOM
OPEN/START:20:00 CLOSE24:00
TICKETS:ADV¥4000(IN TAX/WITHOUT 1DRINK ORDER)
DOOR¥4500(IN TAX/WITHOUT 1DRINK ORDER)
YOU MUST BE 20 AND OVER WITH PHOTO ID

TICKET PIA 0570-02-9999 P-code:242-563
LAWSON TICKET 0570-06-9003 L-code:37472
DISK UNION SHIBUYA CLUB MUSIC SHOP 03-3476-2627
CISCO TECHNO SHOP 03-3496-7038
TECHNIQUE 03-5458-4143
e+ http://eplus.jp/
LIQUIDROOM

INFO:LIQUIDROOM 03-5464-0800 WWW.LIQUIDROOM.NET

SUPPORTED BY TRI-MIX

イベント告知ポスター /
EVENT ANNOUNCEMENT POSTER

リキッドルーム ［クラブ］
LIQUID ROOM ［Live music club］
AD, SB: 浜田武士 Takeshi Hamada

02.4.12.FRIDAY 02.4.12.FRIDAY
SAPPORO SAPPORO
CONCEPT SHOP CONCEPT SHOP
RENEWAL OPEN! RENEWAL OPEN!

ショップリニューアルオープン告知ポスター /
SHOP RENEWAL OPEN ANNOUNCEMENT POSTER

アディダスジャパン ［スポーツ用品販売代理店］
adidas japan K.K. ［Sportting goods selling agent］
CD: 小松裕行 Hiroyuki Komatsu
AD: 水野学 Manabu Mizuno
D, DF, SB: グッドデザインカンパニー good design company co., ltd.

コンセプトブック / CONCEPT BOOK

リーバイス(R) FLU ［アパレル］
Levi's(R)FLU ［Apparel］
CD, AD: 川上 俊　Shun Kawakami
D: 櫻井ユウキ　Yu-ki Sakurai
P: 山田伊久磨　Ikuma Yamada
I: ウラタダシ　Tadashi Ura / ヨザ　Yoza
DF, SB: アートレス　artless Inc.

フリーペーパー / FREE PAPER

ナイキジャパン ［アパレル］
NIKE JAPAN ［Apparel］
CD: 神谷幸之助　Kounosuke Kamitani
AD: ジーノ・ウー　Gino Woo
D: 富山庄太郎　Shotaro Tomiyama
CW: 岩井俊介　Shunsuke Iwai / 尚師喜和子　Kiwako Takashi
ART BUYER: 飯田昭雄　Akio Iida
ACCOUNT: 湯河テッド　Ted Yukawa / シグ セング　Shig Seng
SB: ワイデン＋ケネディ トウキョウ　Wieden + Kennedy Tokyo

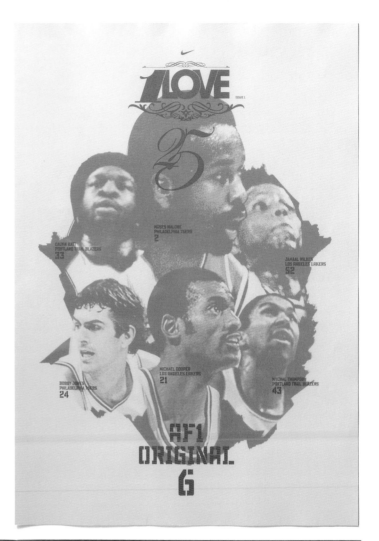

フリーペーパー / FREE PAPER

ナイキジャパン ［アパレル］
NIKE JAPAN ［Apparel］
CD: 神谷幸之助　Kounosuke Kamitani
AD: ジーノ・ウー　Gino Woo
D: 富山庄太郎　Shotaro Tomiyama
CW: 岩井俊介　Shunsuke Iwai / 尚師喜和子　Kiwako Takashi
ART BUYER: 飯田昭雄　Akio Iida
ACCOUNT: 湯河テッド　Ted Yukawa / シグ セング　Shig Seng
SB: ワイデン＋ケネディ トウキョウ　Wieden + Kennedy Tokyo

WE ARE ALL WITNESSES

We've moved through the 11 years history. It is the beginning of the next challenge. Fight together to get the brilliant victory!

Consadole Sapporo
Full Season Pass 2007

ブランドポスター ／ BRAND POSTER

ナイキジャパン［アパレル］
NIKE JAPAN ［Apparel］
ECD: 佐藤澄子 Sumiko Sato / 米村 浩 Hiroshi Yonemura
AD, CW: クリス ハッチンソン Chris Hutchinson /
ドリスコル リード Driscoll Reid
P: ジェフ レイデル Jeff Riedel
ART BUYER: 渋谷浩美 Hiromi Shibuya
ACCOUNT: 湯河テッド Ted Yukawa / シグ セング Shig Seng
SB: ワイデン＋ケネディ トウキョウ Wieden + Kennedy Tokyo

シーズンチケット ／ SEASON TICKET

北海道フットボールクラブ［スポーツチーム］
HOKKAIDO FOOTBALL CLUB ［Sport team］
AD, D, SB: 上田亮 RYO UEDA
P: 小助川拓人 TAKUTO KOSUKEGAWA
DF: コミューングラフィックス COMMUNE GRAPHICS

イベント新聞広告 / NEWSPAPER AD FOR EVENT

パブリックビューイング実行委員会 ［団体］
PUBLIC VIEWING COMMITTEE [Association]
CD: 高松聡　Satoshi Takamatsu
AD, D: 野尻大作　Daisaku Nojiri
CW: 渡辺潤平　Junpei Watanabe
DF, SB: ground　ground

巨人軍は不滅か。

かつて巨人軍は永久に不滅だと言った男が
いた。1億人が感動した。1億人がそう信じた。
しかし、いま僕たちは思う。はたして巨人軍
は不滅なのか。類い稀な才能を持つ男たち
が、懸命に努力を重ねて築き上げた巨人軍
の栄光は守られているだろうか。そのプレー
は全力なのか。そのプレーは自分の限界に
挑戦しているのか。そのプレーは人を感動
させられるのか。そして、巨人軍のメンバー
であることを忘れてはいないか。いま巨人軍
は挑戦者へと変革をしなければならない。
勝つために。感動を与えるために。愛される
ために。そして、永久に不滅の巨人軍である
ために。僕たちは、強い巨人を待っている。

巨人が再び巨人になるのは不可能か。

IMPOSSIBLE IS NOTHING

巨人が再び巨人になるのは不可能か。

IMPOSSIBLE IS NOTHING

巨人軍選手
に告ぐ。

そのプレーは全力なのか。
そのプレーは自分の限界に挑戦しているのか。
そのプレーはごまかしはないのか。
そのプレーは人を感動させられるのか。
そのプレーは巨人軍のメンバーとして誇れるものか。
僕たちは、強い巨人を待っている。

巨人が再び巨人になるのは不可能か。

IMPOSSIBLE IS NOTHING

ブランド新聞広告 ／ BRANDING NEWSPAPER AD

アディダス ジャパン ［スポーツ用品販売代理店］	
adidas Japan K.K. ［Sporting goods selling agent］	
CD, CW: 高松 聡　Satoshi Takamatsu	
AD: 野尻大作　Daisaku Nojiri	
D: 戸崎正浩　Masahiro Tozaki ／ 安達明日香　Asuka Adachi	
P: 瀧本幹也　Mikiya Takimoto	
AGENCY & PLANINNG: 電通　DENTSU Inc.	
AGENCY & PLANINNG, DF, SB: ground　ground	

店舗設計、ショッピングバッグ /
SHOP DESIGN, SHOPPING BAG

ユニクロ ［アパレル］
UNIQLO CO.,LTD. [Apparel]
CD, AD: グエナエル ニコラ　Gwenael Nicolas
D: 水野 薫　Kaoru Mizuno
DF: キュリオシティ　Curiosity Inc.
SB: ユニクロ　UNIQLO CO.,LTD.

MENを極める。

綿を極める。

THE GUNZE

綿を極める。
MENを極める。

THE GUNZE

店頭ポスター、パッケージ /
STORE POSTER, PACKAGE

グンゼ [衣料品]	
GUNZE [Apparel]	
ECD: 塩出芳樹	Yoshiki Shiode
CD, CW: 中尾孝年	Takatoshi Nakao
AD: 堀内弘誓 Hirochika Horiuchi / 福森正紀 Masaki Fukumori	
AD, D: 西谷圭介 Keisuke Nishitani	
D: 木村仁美 Hitomi Kimura	
P: 森山智彦 Tomohiko Moriyama	
ST: 鈴木ちあき Chiaki Suzuki	
PT: アートファクトリー art factory	
DF: 電通関西支社 DENTSU INC. KANSAI	
DF, SB: スリーアンドコー Three & co.	

ADVAN. The leader in our product line-up. The name found only on our top-performing tires. Fast. Comfortable. Genuine. Spirited. ADVAN is for those satisfied only when leading the p...

Not for Everyone. For those who know real performance.

ブランドポスター、ブックレット /
BRANDING POSTER, BOOKLET

横浜ゴム［タイヤメーカー］
The Yokohama Rubber Company, Limited ［Tire manufacturer］
AD: 永井裕明　Hiroaki Nagai
D: 栗原幸治　Koji Kurihara
P: 羽金和恭　Kazuyasu Hagane
CW: 倉橋洋樹　Hiroki Kurahashi
PR: 金尾泰雄　Yasuo Kanao
DF, SB: エヌ・ジー　N.G.INC.

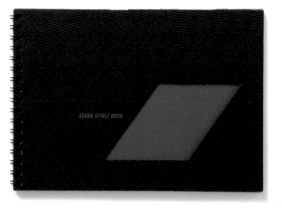

商品案内ポスター ／ PRODUCT PROMOTION POSTER

本田技研工業　[自動車メーカー]	
Honda Motor Co.,Ltd.　[Auto manufactures]	
ECD: 元井康夫　Yasuo Motoi	
SCD: 森本肇　Hajime Morimoto	
CD, AD: 水口克夫　Katsuo Mizuguchi	
AD, D: 野尻大作　Daisaku Nojiri	
D: 戸崎正浩　Masahiro Tozaki ／ 安達明日香　Asuka Adachi	
P: 北井博也　Hiroya Kitai	
CW: 照井晶博　Akihiro Terui	
AGENCY & PLANINNG: 電通　DENTSU Inc. ／ シンガタ　Shingata ／	
風とバラッド　KAZE TO BALLAD INC.	
DF, AGENCY & PLANINNG, SB: ground　ground	

アーティスト ライブツアーグッズ /
ARTIST LIVE TOUR GOODS

ファウンテン [プロダクション]
FOUNTAIN [Theatrical agency]
AD, D: 野尻大作　Daisaku Nojiri
DF: ground　ground

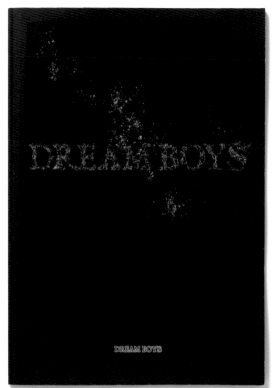

STORY

これは、一本の映画と出会ったことにより、次から次へと運命が
狂わされていった三人の若者たちの物語である。

ボクサーを目指していたコウキはその夢を叶え、チャンピオンにまで
なった。だが、それがきっかけとなった。たったひとりの肉親である弟の康
いる複雑を持っていて、身の危険に瀕していたのだ。コウキと肌
に刺まれた時間は次第に少なくなっていく。

そんなコウキに近づいて来たのが、業界の大物、マダム・ビバリ
が経営するオフィスのプロデューサー、マコトだ。マコトはコウキの
弟を集めることに指げ込も何を一切を取り付ける。

ヤクザ師弟したのはアーティストの弟。だが、仲間とユニットを組
んで活動しているのは、思うようにはいっていない。ヤクザは兄
で活動しているコウキの方、主演兼セラ・ユニットに誘われないが
とのこと、しかし、主演条件があった。カズヤに主演をやるような
ヤクザ師弟出来ない、というものだ。

そして、これという理由を見つけることの出来なかったカズヤと
いない。正確に言うと、母親に捨てられたのだ。ショービジネスの

STORY

これは、一本の映画と出会ったことで、次から次へと運命が狂わされていった三人の若者たちの物語である。

This is the story of three young men whose lives became havoc changed by their relationship to a movie.

演劇パンフレット ／ THEATRICAL BROCHURE

エム。シィオー。［出版社］
M.Co. [Publisher]
CD: Jet State Inc.   Jet State Inc.
AD, D, DF, SB : Hd Lab Inc.   Hd Lab Inc.
P: ゴー・リッラクス・イー・モア   go relax E more
WEAR STYLIST: 石黒亮一   Ryouichi Ishiguro
PROP STYLIST: 石崎 純   Jun Ishizaki

We can live this life just once,
so why don't we make something happen?
If you have time to search the reason,
just put your right hand up stronger in the air instead!

I have struck by rain, got damaged. Breathing with just sadness and pain.

Kazuya Kamenashi *as Kazuari*

DREAM BOYS

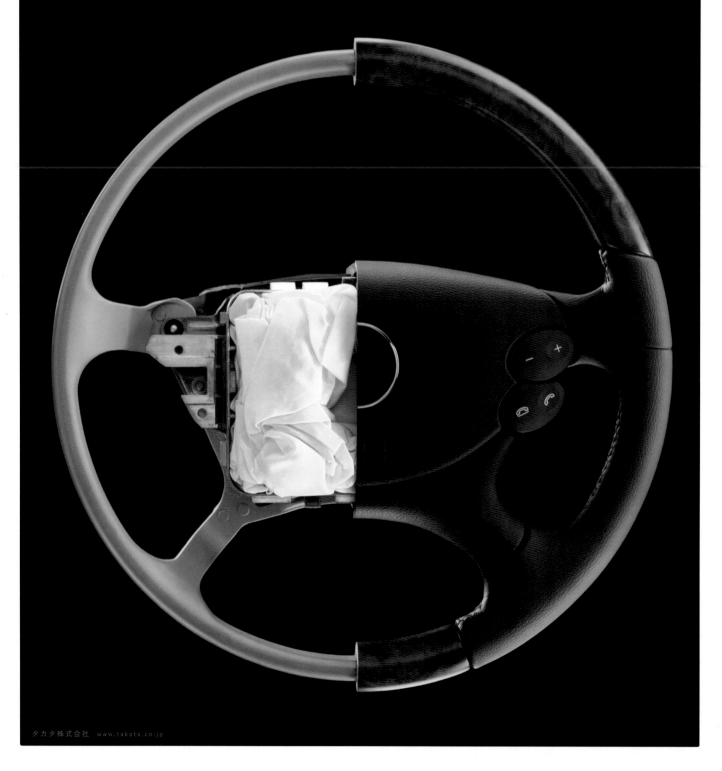

わたしは、タカタです。ステアリングを握ることは、安全装置を握ること。中心のパッド内に、エアバッグをきちんと小さく折りたたみ、でも、いざという瞬間、最大限に膨らむように収納します。ステアリングには、エアバッグが内側にあることを意識させないデザインと安全性の両立。線路を集中させる高い技術が必要です。タカタは、マグネシウムダイキャスト・フレームなどの最先端技術を駆使しながら、安全装置としてのステアリングシステムを世界のカーメーカーに提供しています。タカタがめざすのは、交通事故の犠牲者がゼロになる日。その日を信じて、厳しい品質基準を定め、最率をクリアできる製品だけをつくっています。チャイルドシートもまったく同じ。やさしいデザインの内側にあるのは、研ぎ澄まされた安全技術です。◎チャイルドシートのカタログをさしあげます。下記のホームページからご請求ください。

TAKATA

タカタ株式会社　www.takata.co.jp

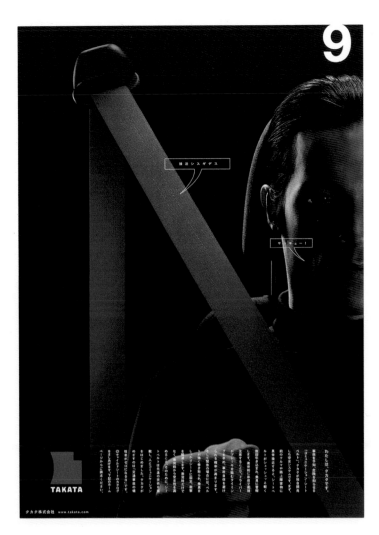

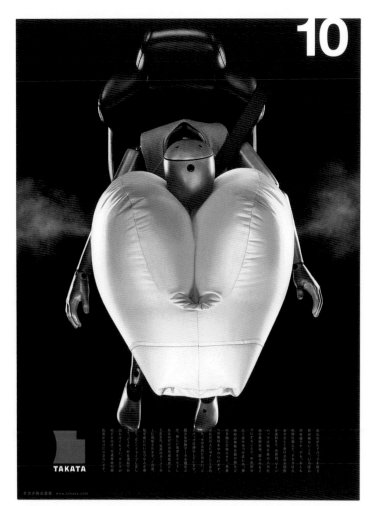

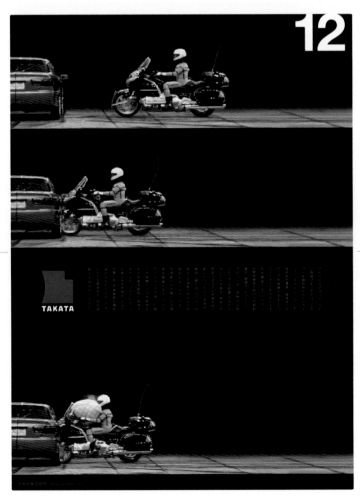

企業ブランド新聞広告 /
COMPANY NEWSPAPER AD

タカタ [製品メーカー]
TAKATA [Product manufacture]
CD: 神谷幸之助　Kounosuke Kamitani
AD: 日髙英輝　Eiki Hidaka
D: 相田俊一　Shunichi Aita
P: 岡田初彦　Hatsuhiko Okada
CW: 名雪祐平　Yuhei Nayuki
SB: グリッツデザイン　gritzdesign inc.

RIDE
ON THE TOMAMU

TOMAMU
ALPHA RESORT

ブランドポスター / BRANDING POSTER

星野リゾート・トマム　[リゾート施設運営]
HOSHINO RESORT TOMAMU　[Resort facility management]
CD, CW: 所俊彦　TOSHIHIKO TOKORO
AD, D, SB: 上田亮　RYO UEDA
P: 佐藤整　HITOSHI SATO
DF: コミューングラフィックス　COMMUNE GRAPHICS

シーズンチケット / SEASON TICKET

東北楽天ゴールデンイーグルス　[野球チーム]
TOHOKU RAKUTEN GOLDEN EAGLES　[Baseball team]
AD, D, SB: 上田亮　RYO UEDA
P: 小助川拓人　TAKUTO KOSUKEGAWA
DF: コミューングラフィックス　COMMUNE GRAPHICS

RUGBY FOOTBALL
2001 SEASON OPENING MATCH.
JAPAN × PRESIDENT'S XV
09.07 FRI. 2001 19:00 KICK OFF   AT 国立競技場

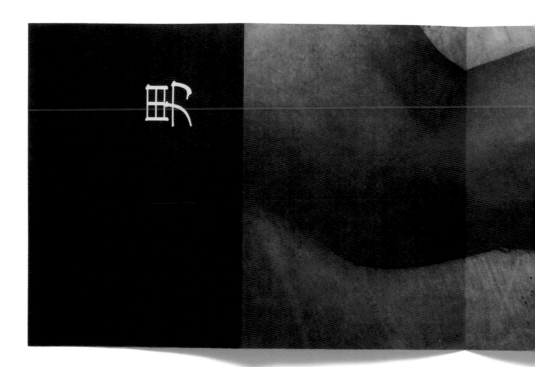

20**01** SEPTEMBER

INTRODUC-
ING THE
SCHEDULE
OF RUGBY
FOOTBALL
MATCHES.

09

競技大会告知ポスター、リーフレット /
**SPORT COMPETITION ANNOUNCEMENT POSTER,
LEAFLET**

日本ラグビーフットボール協会 [団体]
All Japan Rugby Foot Ball Association [Association]
CD: 柴田常文 Tsunefumi Shibata
AD, D: 佐野研二郎 Kenjiro Sano
D: 杉山ユキ Yuki Sugiyama
CW: 菱谷信浩 Nobuhiro Hishiya
P: 薄井一護 Ichigo Usui
SB: 博報堂 HAKUHODO INC. / MR_DESIGN MR_DESIGN

RUGBY FOOTBALL
PREMIER CHALLENGE 2002.
SUNTORY × SARACENS (FROM ENGLAND)
8.25 TUE 19:00 KICK OFF AT 国立競技場

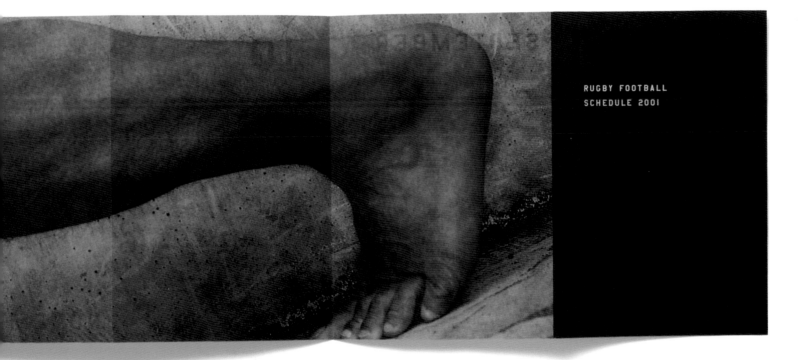

RUGBY FOOTBALL
SCHEDULE 2001

JAPAN
RUGBY FOOTBALL
CHAMPIONSHIP

SCHEDULE

OCTOBER

NOVEMBER 11

DECEMBER 12

ACCESS + TELEPHONE

JAPAN RUGBY FOOTBALL UNION　(財)日本ラグビーフットボール協会　03-3401-3290

職業：柔道家
吉田秀彦

缶コーヒーと
男は、
ちょっと
甘めがいい。

商品案内ポスター、雑誌広告 /
PRODUCT PROMOTION POSTER, MAGAZINE AD

ポッカコーポレーション [飲料、食料品の製造販売、仕入販売他]
Pokka corporation [Beverage Production and Sales]
CD, CW: 黒田康嗣　Yasushi Kuroda
AD: 秋山具義　Gugi Akiyama
D: 八木ひとみ　Hitomi Yagi
P: 若木信吾　Shingo Wakagi / 大橋仁　Jin Ohashi
DF, SB: デイリー・フレッシュ　Dairy Fresh

Judo

2003 World Judo Championships

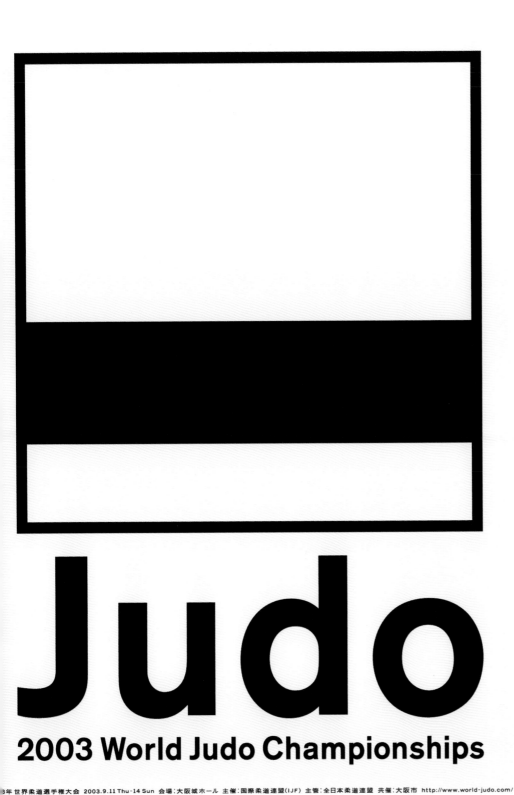

Judo

2003 World Judo Championships

3年 世界柔道選手権大会 2003.9.11 Thu-14 Sun 会場：大阪城ホール 主催：国際柔道連盟(IJF) 主管：全日本柔道連盟 共催：大阪市 http://www.world-judo.com/

競技大会告知ポスター／
SPORT COMPETITION ANNOUNCEMENT POSTER

全日本柔道連盟 ［団体］
All Japan Judo Federation ［Association］
CD: 千葉 篤 Atsushi Chiba
AD, D: 佐野研二郎 Kenjiro Sano
D: 武田利一 Toshikazu Takeda
CW: 斉藤賢司 Kenji Saito
SB: 博報堂 HAKUHODO INC. / MR_DESIGN MR_DESIGN

１００年、星 を見上げ た 。　　　　　　１００年、夢をみた。

商品案内ポスター ／ PRODUCT PROMOTION POSTER

アサヒ飲料 ［飲料製造・販売］
ASAHI SOFT DRINKS CO.,Ltd ［Beverage Supplies］
CD: 勝田泰二　Yasuji Katsuta
AD, D: 戸田宏一郎　Koichiro Toda
D: 渡辺亮　Ryo Watanabe
CW: 忽那治郎　Jiro Kotsuna
SB: 株式会社電通　DENTSU INC.

アミューズメント施設案内ポスター ／
AMUSEMENT GROUNDS PROMOTION POSTER

富士急行 ［レジャー産業］
FUJIKYUKO CO.,LTD ［Leisure industry］
CD: 勝田泰二　Yasuji Katsuta
AD: 戸田宏一郎　Koichiro Toda
D: 石田沙綾子　Sayako Ishida
CW: 志伯健太郎　Kentaro Shihaku
SB: 電通　DENTSU INC.

100 年、愛し つづけ た　　　 。

たどりついたブラック。　100年 BLACK

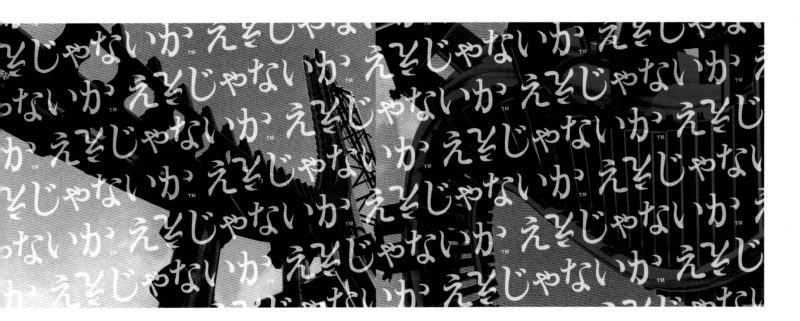

TUROE 移ROE
SONO 席DE 飲MIAKASE

live style cafe for night people. tanabe wakayama UTuBoMu-N

REZURE
NARU 儘NI
夜NO OKUE 奥ETO

live style cafe for night people. tanabe wakayama UTuBoMu-N

ROBORONI 酔U 死ZUKASHISATO 晴REGAMASHISA

live style cafe for night people. tanabe wakayama UTuBoMu-N

ブランドポスター / BRANDING POSTER

ウツボムーン ［ライブハウス］
Utsubo-Moon ［Live music club］
AD, D: 永井裕明　Hiroaki Nagai
D: 高橋かおる　Kaoru Takahashi / 中井昌典　Masanori Nakai
P: 藤井保　Tamotsu Fujii
CW: 藤原大作　Daisaku Fujiwara
ARTIST: 豊嶋敦史　Atsushi Toyoshima
DF, SB: エヌ・ジー　N.G.INC.,

ANA 時KANNI ICHI秒 GOTONI
向KAIAU KYō楽

live style cafe for night people. tanabe wakayama UTuBoMu-N

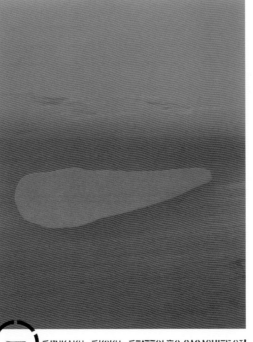

番FUKAKU一番KOKU一番TATTOI 夜O SAGASHITE SA!

live style cafe for night people. tanabe wakayama UTuBoMu-N

OONGA 若REREBA
MOON WA 涼KABU

UTuBoMnN

live style cafe for night people. tanabe wakayama UTuBoMu-N

Aquatics Archery Athletics Air Sports Automobile Badminton Baseball Basketball Boxing Biathlon Bobsleigh Bandy Boules Billiard Sports Bowling Bridge Canoe Cycling Curling Chess DanceSport E
Football Gymnastics Golf Handball Hockey Ice Hockey Judo Kayak Karate Korfball Luge Life Saving Motorcycle Racing Mountaineering and Climbing Modern Pentathlon Netball Orienteering Pelote Basqu
Roller Sports Rugby Rowing Sailing Shooting Softball Skating Skiing Squash Surfing Table Tennis Taekwondo Tennis Triathlon Tug of War Underwater Sports Volleyball Weightlifting Wrestling Water

スポーツのライバルは乳酸だった。対乳酸にはクエン酸。

商品案内ポスター、パッケージ /
PRODUCT PROMOTON POSTER, PACKAGE

キリンビバレッジ ［飲料製造・販売］
Kirin Beverage Company,Limited. ［Beverage Supplies］
CD, AD: 水野 学　Manabu Mizuno
CD, CW: 東 秀紀　Hideki Azuma
D, DF, SB: グッドデザインカンパニー　good design company co., ltd.

パッケージ / PACKAGE

伊勢醤油本舗 [醤油製造]
Ise Syoyu Honpo [Soy sauce manufacturer]
CD, D: 三浦正紀　Masanori Miura
SB: パブリックデザインワークス　PUBLIC DESIGN WORKS INC.

ブランドポスター / BRANDING POSTER

山崎文栄堂 [コンサルティング会社]
Yamazaki Bun-eidou [Consulting Company]
AD, D: 居山浩二　Koji Iyama
DF, SB: イヤマデザイン　iyamadesign

ACTIVE

Vigorous / Youthful / Naughty
元気な / 溌剌とした / 腕白な

Daisaku Nojiri —"tough" designer talks about "tough-style" design

"A strong message that reaches the target market" is the absolute minimum requirement when designing advertising. Japanese consumers tend not to be fond of the in-your-face "edgy" approach, and so that type of straight-pitching advertising ends up without a target audience. I think a message that reaches everyone, a message that is "functional," regardless of your nationality or whether you're a man or a woman, is what good design is all about. It's not a question of deciding between "cute" design or "cool" design, what's important is that, whichever you choose, it properly conveys a sense of the product. The style you are seeing now is the result of researching better ways to communicate with consumers.

When I choose black

I use black when I want to put forth a strong, unequivocal message.

DAISAKU NOJIRI

Art director and graphic designer

Born 1975 in Yokohama. In 1999, he joined C.C. Lemon, and in 2005 participated in setting up Ground. Among the many honors he has received are the NY ADC Award, the JAGDA the New Designer Award, the Mayor of the City of Brno Award at the International Biennale of Graphic Design Brno, admission to the Chaumont Poster Festival, the Korea International Poster Biennale Bronze, and the Clio Award. He art directs works in genres ranging from major campaigns to book and CD jackets, and fashion.

His Works / P29, P36-37, P42-43, P68-69, P104-107, P136-137, P159, P180-181, 184

『男』なデザイナーの語る『男』なデザイン／野尻大作

「強い表現であること」は広告をデザインする上で最低限満たしていなければならない要素です。直球な広告こそターゲットレス。国籍も性差も関係ない。そんな誰にでも伝わる、"機能する" 表現こそ、良いデザインだと思います。カワイイ表現にするか、カッコいい表現にするかの選択ではなく、どちらが商品を正しく伝えられるかが重要。より伝わる方法論を追求した結果のデザインであることが大切だと考えています。

黒を選ぶとき

色でごまかさない強いメッセージを主張したいときに選びます。

野尻大作

1975年横浜生まれ。1999年C.C.レマン入社。05年グラウンドの設立に参加。NY.ADC賞、JAGDA新人賞、ブルノ国際ポスタービエンナーレブルノ市長賞、グラフィックデザインビエンナーレ、ショーモンポスターフェスティバル、韓国ポスタービエンナーレ、米国クリオ賞など受賞多数。メジャーキャンペーンから、装丁、CDジャケット、ファンションまで幅広い分野でアートディレクションを行う。

作品掲載ページ／P29, P36-37, P42-43, P68-69, P104-107, P136-137, P159, P180-181, 184

HE

PHOTOGRAPHY
HASSE NIELSEN
STYLING
DANIEL MAGNUSSEN

FAL
LING

FOR
WARD

LOOK

JIL
SANDER

This season, you either cut the crap and go right to the structural core of things, or you reserve the right to self-indulge. There is no in-between. You might think that simplicity is the easiest way to go when it comes to clothes, but one look at Raf Simons for Jil Sander tells you there is so much more to it. Minimalism has always been a trademark for Jil Sander, but this time it's taken to a whole new level. There is nothing left but the absolute essential, the monochrome colorfields of orange, grey and blue. The shapes, reduced to squares and triangles, almost render the body dispensable. Prada follows the same path. It might be the road to the future, or space. It surely leads us somewhere new. This season also offers versions of timeless luxury. Yves Saint Laurent and Burberry Prorsum presented us with clothing that has historical references, ranging from the twenties to the nineties, but the overall look is more about feeling good in general—loose pants, sandals, highly tactile fabrics and soft palettes. This classic notion of opulence is a theme at Comme des Garçons, who presented a collection almost entirely covered in gold. Talk about surplus. But as it is Comme, it never got tacky or too bling-bling. The tired feeling that you sensed a few seasons back seems to have evaded designers, and we are once again seeing collections that present new views on modern masculinity. On these pages, we show you some of our favorites. TEXT FREDERIK LARSEN

PHOTOGRAPHY
JOHN SCARISBRICK
STYLING
DANIEL MAGNUSSEN

CHAIR
MAN

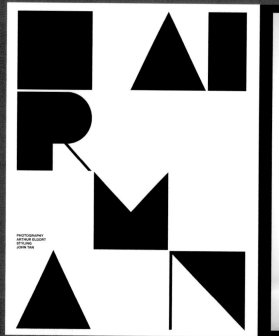

PHOTOGRAPHY
ARTHUR ELGORT
STYLING
JOHN TAN

CHRISTMA

男性誌 / MEN'S MAGAZINE

HE magazine [雑誌]
HE magazine [Magazine]
AD, D, SB: homework

THE MAGAZINE
ALL FASHION
FASCINATION
WINTER 2006
/2007

106 HE

WORK IN PROGRESS

Ezra Petronio and Suzanne Koller are the creative team behind Work in Progress, a Paris-based creative agency that works with blue-chip fashion clients like Miu Miu, Prada, and Chloé. They also produce Self Service: the hardcover, bi-annual style bible that sets the tone, season after season, for how fashion is interpreted by the rest of us. Koller and Petronio witnessed the genesis of a new legion of European talent – Hedi Simane, Raf Simons, David Sims and Nicolas Ghesquière among its ranks – that ushered in daring ideas about contemporary fashion.

Petronio and Koller supported these vanguards in both commercial and editorial capacities; hand-in-hand, this fresh generation of creatives transmogrified the industry. Everything they produce,

from brand identities to printed matter, is packaged colorfully and artfully, in a mélange of mismatched fonts and on numerous paper stocks. Over the past decade plus some, this has changed the face of fashion—something often said, but in their case irrefutably true.

Over the phone from his office at 7 rue Debelleyme, Petronio gave HE a candid account of his motiv-ations for leaving New York years ago, his recent projects with Work in Progress, why he loves his Polaroid Big Shot and what frustrates him most about Paris. With luck, the next generation will have this guy around to make their brands (and their portraits) look as gorgeous as his own.
TEXT KATE SENNERT

Kate Sennert: I'd like to start with the basics. When did you meet your working partner Suzanne Koller? What is your company Work in Progress all about?
Ezra Petronio: I met Suzanne Koller about 20 years ago. She was also an art director and graphic designer, and we started Work in Progress 14 years ago (in 1993). It began as a design agency before *Self Service* happened. We'd both worked at different magazines and studios before. We started the magazine two years later, so it's about 12 years old. It's not like we're magazine people who also do consulting; our main job is graphic design and advertising. We've grown very organically over the years by accumulating encounters and experiences, whether they are through the magazine or with different generations of [fashion] designers.

Kate: Who are some of your clients? What have you been working on lately?
Ezra: We've worked with a lot of different designers including Phoebe Philo and Muccia Prada. For the past six seasons we've been doing overall brand art direction with Miu Miu. We oversee all creative direction for the brand, meaning we work on every aspect from the advertising campaigns to the website to catalogs. We've also been doing a lot of stuff for Prada; we actually started working for Prada before Miu Miu. We've been collaborating with [Muccia Prada] for a long time, on lots of very special things. For example, when they opened the store in Aoyama and when they did the ephemeral store for Art Basel we collaborated on the communication. We've come up with a lot of copywriting for her, along with special packaging. We

also started working a lot with Prada beauty, which has been a big, big client. And more recently, Prada fragrance. That's a great example of a very complete project: the bottle, the packaging, the campaign, everything. Another one of my clients is Chloé, which we've followed for eight seasons. That's overall brand art direction, meaning image, positioning and strategy. So, as an art director you get to work on all aspects, which is the fun part of the job. It pushes you to express all the different mediums in which you can work.
Kate: What was the catalyst for starting *Self Service*?
We have always been passionate about magazines. It's something that I've taken from the high school newspaper. When I was at Parsons, I worked at *Interview*, and I also worked for magazines in Paris. Suzanne was working at *Glamour* when we met.

フューチャーマーケティングサミット事務局 ［団体］
Future Marketing Summit Tokyo [Association]
AD, D, SB: 長嶋りかこ　Rikako Nagashima
D: 水溜友絵　Tomoe Mizutamari
P: 青山たかかず　Takakazu Aoyama
CW: 大八木翼　Tsubasa Oyagi
DF: シロップ　Syrup
PR: 星本和容　Kazuhiro Hoshimoto

「広告の未来を熱く話し合うサミット」というコンセプトを表現
するため、燃え上がって焼けこげたような加工を施している。

A burn-mark-like effect adorns the promotional pieces for a summit
seeking heated discussion about the future of marketing.

ABAHOUSE

シーズンビジュアル、ノベルティ（バンダナ）、カタログ /
**SEASON VISUAL, NOVELTY (BAN・DAN・NA),
CATALOGUE**

アバハウスインターナショナル ［アパレル］
ABAHOUSE INTERNATIONAL CO. [Apparel]
AD, D: 野尻大作　Daisaku Nojiri
P: 北井博也(シーズンビジュアル)　Hiroya Kitai (Season visual) /
　　樋口兼一(カタログ)　Kenichi Higuchi (Catalogue)
DF, SB: ground　ground

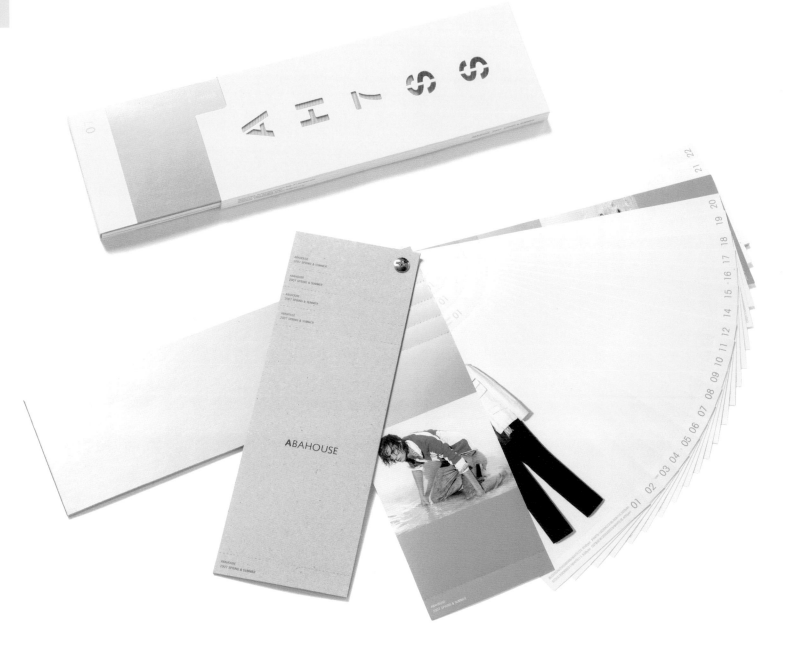

Grand
Bazar
1.17 thu - 21 mon

Laforet

イベント告知ポスター、店頭POP、ショップバッグ、メガホン／
EVENT ANNOUNCEMENT POSTER,
STORE POSTER, SHOP BAG, MEGAPHONE

ラフォーレ原宿 [商業施設]
Laforet [Commercial Facility]
CD, AD, D, SB: 長嶋りかこ　Rikako Nagashima
D: 水溜友絵　Tomoe Mizutamari / 本田絵梨　Eri Honda /
　　石橋絵理　Eri Ishibashi / 中尾宏美　Hiromi Nakao
P: Miko Lim
DF: シロップ　Syrup
STYLIST: TAKAO
MAKE: Yuki
HAIR: 西村浩一　Koichi Nishimura
PR: 星本和容　Kazuhiro Hoshimoto

キャンペーンポスター ／ CAMPAIGN POSTER

日本コカ・コーラ ［清涼飲料の製造販売］
Coca-Cola (Japan) Company, Limited [Beverage Production and Sales]
CD: 田中徹　Toru Tanaka
AD: 加藤建吾　Kengo Kato
D: 新井崇　Takashi Arai / 竹中智博　Tomohiro Takenaka /
　　山田靖子　Yasuko Yamada / 草野剛　Tsuyoshi Kusano /
　　宮崎貴年　Takatoshi Miyazaki / 前沢暢之　Nobuyuki Maezawa
P: シュウ　アカシ　Shu Akashi
CW: 上田浩和　Hirokazu Ueda / 花井智　Satoshi Hanai
PR: 沼井秀樹　Hideki Numai / 三ツ橋憲司　Kenji Mitsuhashi
DF, SB: タグボートツー　TUGBOAT2

商品案内ポスター /
PRODUCT PROMOTION POSTER

麒麟麦酒 [酒類製造・販売]
Kirin Brewery Company, Limited [Sales & production of alchol beverages]
CD: 千葉 篤　Atsushi Chiba / 滝川修志　Kiyoshi Takigawa
AD, D, SB: 長嶋りかこ　Rikako Nagashima
D: 水溜友絵　Tomoe Mizutamari
P: 青山たかかず　Takakazu Aoyama
CW: 木村元紀　Genki Kimura
DF: シロップ　Syrup
PR: 星本和容　Kazuhiro Hoshimoto
DIGITAL ARTIST: 吉川武志　Takeshi Yoshikawa /
　　　　　　　上野慶介　Keisuke Ueno

空間演出 / SPACE DIRECTION

資生堂　[化粧品の製造・販売]
Shiseido CO.,LTD.　[Cosmetics Manufacture&Sales]
CD: 山本浩司　Koji Yamamoto
AD, D: 丸橋 桂　Katsura Marubashi
CW: 村澤浩昭　Hiroaki Murasawa
P: 中西隆良　Takayoshi Nakanishi
SB: 資生堂　Shiseido CO.,LTD.

パッケージ / PACKAGE

資生堂　[化粧品の製造・販売]
Shiseido CO.,LTD.　[Cosmetics Manufacture&Sales]
CD, AD: 松永 真　Shin Matsunaga
CD: 山本浩司　Koji Yamamoto
AD: 菊池泰輔　Taisuke Kikuchi
D: 松永真次郎　Shinjiro Matsunaga ／ 駒井麻郎　Mao Komai
DF: 松永真デザイン事務所　Shin Matsunaga Design Inc.
SB: 資生堂　Shiseido CO.,LTD.

店舗設計、パッケージ / SHOP DESIGN, PACKAGE

ユニクロ [アパレル]
UNIQLO CO.,LTD. [Apparel]
CD, AD: 佐藤可士和　Kashiwa Sato
AD: MARKUS KIERSZTAN
D: 石川耕　Ko Ishikawa
INTERIOR DESIGNER: 入川英人　Hideto Irikawa
DF: サムライ　SAMURAI Inc.

UNIQLO PAPER N°1

FROM TOKYO TO NEW YORK

ISSUE 1   FREE COPY

THE NEW FACE OF UNIQLO
CREATED BY KASHIWA SATO

UNIQLO REGULAR

FROM TOKYO TO NEW YORK FROM TOKYO TO NEW YORK
FROM TOKYO TO NEW YORK FROM TOKYO TO NEW YORK
FROM TOKYO TO NEW YORK FROM TOKYO TO
FROM TOKYO TO NEW YORK FROM TOKYO TO
FROM TOKYO TO NEW YORK FROM TOKYO T
FROM TOKYO TO NEW YORK FRO
FROM TOKYO TO NEW YOR
FROM TOKYO TO NEW
FROM TOKYO TO

UNIQLO BOLD

FROM TOKYO TO NEW YORK FROM TOKYO TO NEW YORK
FROM TOKYO TO NEW YORK FROM TOKYO TO NEW YORK
FROM TOKYO TO NEW YORK FROM TOKYO TO NEW YORK
FROM TOKYO TO NEW YORK FROM TOKYO T
FROM TOKYO TO NEW YORK FRO
FROM TOKYO TO NEW YOR
FROM TOKYO TO NEW YOR
FROM TOKYO TO NEW
FROM TOKYO TO NEW
FROM TOKYO TO

FALL/WINTER 2006

IN THIS ISSUE
FALL/WINTER 2006

UNIQLO INTERNATIONAL
Nice to meet you.

THE UNIQUBE
Sport meets street.
Photographer
Magnus Unnar
page 8

I LOVE NEW YORK
What's not to love?
Writing
Glenn O'Brien
page 15

ODE TO UNIQLO
Behind the glitz
and gloss.
Writing
Kyoichi Tsuzuki
page 17

THE JEANS
ARE ALL RIGHT!
Japanese
premium denim.
Photographer
Ben Pogue
page 18

THE GIRL
FROM GRAMERCY
Parkside elegance.
Photographer
KT Auleta
page 20

Q&A
KIM GORDON
The art of music.
Interview
Matthew Eberhart
page 28

MONOQLO:
WHITE OUT!
Your best
winter whites.
Photographer
Ben Pogue
page 30

GHOST IN THE SHIRT
Is this wardrobe
haunted?
Photographer
Bela Borsodi
page 32

STAIRWAY TO DENIM
The man behind
UNIQLO's global
flagship design.
Interview
Chako Yoshiie
page 40

HOW WOULD
YOU WEAR IT?
Streetstyle showdown:
Williamsburg vs.
Harajuku.
Photographer
Vincent Skeltis
page 43

FROM JAPAN
WITH LOVE
Japanese Pop Culture
T-Shirt Project.
Photographer
Kenneth Cappello
page 48

Q&A
MASAHARU
MORIMOTO
Iron chef and
restaurateur
extraordinaire.
Interview
Leigh Stevens
page 56

OUR NEW
FALL COLORS
Hues for the season.
Photographer
Ben Pogue
page 58

TOYS WILL BE TOYS
Stuffed yet
sophisticated.
Photographer
William Selden
page 60

PERSONAL BEST
Bookseller
William Hall.
Photographer
Kenneth Cappello
page 60

PLUS OR MIN...
Less is mo...
Photographer
Alexei Hay...
page 70

TAKUMI N...
Japanese
textile ma...
Writing
Matt Smith...
page 80

UNIQLO N...
Something...
the wallet...
page 69

STORE LI...
Find us...
page 69

TRANSLA...
Japanese ...
page 80

ISSUE 1   UNIQLO PAPER

THE UNIQUBE

SPORT MEETS STREET AT UNIQLO

ISSUE 1   UNIQLO PAPER

Q

QUITE A NICE T-SHIRT
YOU HAVE ON THERE.
WHERE'S IT FROM?

From Japan With Love

PHOTOGRAPHER   Kenneth Cappello
STYLIST   Christopher Niquet
HAIR AND MAKEUP   Kristen Gallegos

Closer Look

PHOTOGRAPHER   Ben Pogue
PROP STYLIST   Molly Findlay

FALL/WINTER 2006

FROM JAPAN WITH LOVE

ARTIST T-SHIRTS AT UNIQLO

ISSUE 1   UNIQLO PAPER

フリーペーパー / FREE PAPER

ユニクロ ［アパレル］
UNIQLO CO.,LTD. ［Apparel］
CD: 佐藤可士和　Kashiwa Sato
AD: Katia Kuethe / Philipp Muessigmann
D: Sidsel Eriksen / Mkrcel Baer
P: Ben Pogue / Alexei Hay Et. Al
I: Bend Schifferdecker
C: Matt Smith
DF: Studio Von Birken

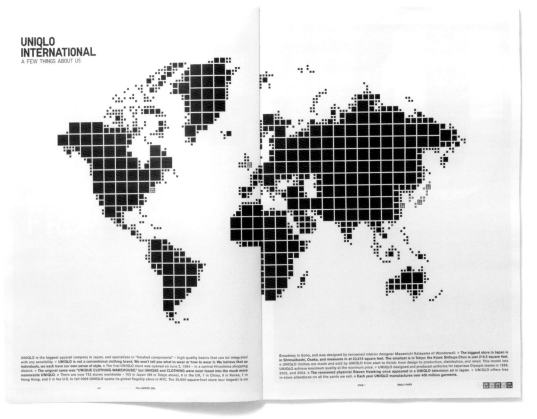

UNIQLO INTERNATIONAL
A FEW THINGS ABOUT US

UNIQLO is the biggest apparel company in Japan, and specializes in "finished components" – high-quality basics that can be integrated with any sensibility. ● UNIQLO is not a conventional clothing brand. We won't tell you what to wear or how to wear it. We believe that as individuals, we each have our own sense of style. ● The first UNIQLO store was opened on June 2, 1984 – in a central Hiroshima shopping district. ● The original name was "UNIQUE CLOTHING WAREHOUSE," but UNIQUE and CLOTHING were soon fused into the much more memorable UNIQLO. ● There are now 733 stores worldwide – 703 in Japan (99 in Tokyo alone), 8 in the UK, 7 in China, 9 in Korea, 1 in Hong Kong, and 6 in the U.S. In fall 2006 UNIQLO opens its global flagship store in NYC. The 35,000-square-foot store (our largest) is on Broadway in Soho, and was designed by renowned interior designer Masamichi Katayama of Wonderwall. ● The biggest store in Japan is in Shinsaibashi, Osaka, and measures in at 23,315 square feet. The smallest is in Tokyo: the Kiosk Shibuya-Chuo is just 215.5 square feet. ● UNIQLO clothes are made and sold by UNIQLO from start to finish: from design to production, distribution, and retail. This model lets UNIQLO achieve maximum quality at the minimum price. ● UNIQLO designed and produced uniforms for Japanese Olympic teams in 1998, 2002, and 2004. ● The renowned physicist Steven Hawking once appeared in a UNIQLO television ad in Japan. ● UNIQLO offers free in-store alterations on all the pants we sell. ● Each year UNIQLO manufactures over 400 million garments.

U

URBAN-INSPIRED SPORT STYLES AND COLORFUL, CUBIC CONSTRUCTIONS. UNIQUE.

The Uniqlo   Closer Look

PHOTOGRAPHER   PHOTOGRAPHER   Bee Pogue
STYLIST   Magnus Unnar   PROP STYLIST   Molly Findlay
                Nicola Formichetti
HAIR   Tomo
MAKEUP   Maki Ryoike

JAPANESE POP CULTURE
T-SHIRT PROJECT
ON THE OCCASION OF UNIQLO'S MOVE TO NEW YORK, WE INVITED SOME OF JAPAN'S MOST INTERESTING DESIGNERS, ARTISTS, FILMMAKERS, AND PHOTOGRAPHERS – FROM THE UP-AND-COMING TO THE LONG-ESTABLISHED – TO CREATE A SPECIAL EDITION UNIQLO T-SHIRT. EACH ARTIST WAS GIVEN TOTAL FREEDOM TO CREATE THE DESIGN THAT BEST EXPRESSED THEIR VISION OF CONTEMPORARY POP CULTURE IN JAPAN. WE WERE VERY HAPPY WITH THE RESULTS, SO WE BROUGHT SOME OF OUR FAVORITES TO 10 DOWNTOWN NEW YORKERS OF ALL CREATIVE TYPES AND HAD THEM TRY THE NEW SHIRTS ON FOR SIZE.

KENNETH is a New York-based photographer from Houston, Texas. Weaned on punk and skate culture, his images have a distinct spontaneity and display a uniquely raw glamour. He's released a book (and is working on another) and recently shot a music video, all while shooting fashion and portraits for a wide range of publications, including this story.
This is his self-portrait.
T-Shirt by Daido Moriyama

DEVIN grew up in Bushwick, Brooklyn, so he's been in NYC pretty much his whole life, save for a year or so he spent in the Poconos hanging out in the woods. Until recently he was studying painting and drawing at Cooper Union, but he decided the academic structure wasn't really doing much for his creativity and split. He's looking for a new studio, and thinking he might even want to look at a few in Berlin.
T-Shirt by Solobongu-Sensei

JAMES became a hairdresser when he lost a bet to a friend. Well, not really, we just thought that sounded good. But he does love his job. After starting in a salon, he now works mostly on photo productions. He says the best part of the job is constantly working with new people, and he thrives on good creative energy coming from others.
T-Shirt by Nobuyoshi Araki

previous page from left to right
Nobuyoshi Araki
Nobuyoshi Araki
Enlightenment

MARLENE is a fine art and fashion photographer who also recently directed her first music video, a rather surreal piece about two girls in a park on a winter picnic for an Arto Lindsay song called "Into Shade." She's looking to continue motion picture projects along with her still photography.
T-Shirt by Atsuki Kikuchi

BILL is a skateboard videographer and writer. Skating alongside some of the best riders out there, he's filmed everything from team videos for various skate companies to documentaries. He basically gets paid to hang out with other skaters. Not bad work if you can get it.
T-Shirt by Wonderwall/Masamichi Katayama

STORE LIST

JAPAN

UNIQLO ASAHIKAWA ASAHIMACHI 7-641-120 ASAHIMACHIJYOU ASAHIKAWA-SHI HOKKAIDO UNIQLO ASAHIKAWA NAGAYAMA 4-1-20 NAGAYAMA ASAHIKAWA-SHI HOKKAIDO UNIQLO ASAHIKAWA TOYOOKA TOYOOKA 4-1-18 TOYOOKA4JYO ASAHIKAWA-SHI HOKKAIDO UNIQLO IWAMIZAWA IWAMIZAWA TOWNPLAZA 4-3-2 YAMATO1JYO IWAMIZAWA-SHI HOKKAIDO UNIQLO KUSHIRO HARUTORI 7-1-48 HARUTORI KUSHIRO-SHI HOKKAIDO UNIQLO KUSHIRO SHIN 3-3-7SHOUWACHUOH KUSHIRO-SHI HOKKAIDO UNIQLO BIBI SAPPORO 9-2-20 HIGASHI-KU KITA1JYOHIGASHI SAPPORO-SHI HOKKAIDO UNIQLO SAPPORO ESTA ESTABILDI TOWNPLAZA HIBARIGAOKA TOWNPLAZA 2-1-2 ATSUBETSU-KU ATSUBETSUCHUOH2JYO SAPPORO-SHI HOKKAIDO UNIQLO SAPPORO ESTA ESTABILDI CHUOH-KU KITA5JYONISHI SAPPORO-SHI HOKKAIDO UNIQLO SAPPORO 1CHUO 4-1CHUOH-KU MINAMI2JYONISHI SAPPORO-SHI HOKKAIDO UNIQLO PORO MIYANOSAWA 5-1-7NISHI-KUMIYANOSAWA1JYO SAPPORO-SHI HOKKAIDO UNIQLO SAPPORO TUMIKAWA MYUNHENOHASHI 22-2-5 TOYOHIRA HIRAGISHI1JYO SAPPORO-SHI HOKKAIDO UNIQLO SAPPORO KYOTA 2-5-6 KIYOTA-KU KIYOTA2JYO SAPPORO-SHI HOKKAIDO UNIQLO SAPPORO KAP SHOPPINGPLAZA KAWAZOE 1-1-60 MINAMI-KUKAWAZOE15JYO SAPPORO-SHI HOKKAIDO UNIQLO SAPPORO TONDEN 4-7-28 KITA-KU TONDEN SAPPORO-SHI HOKKAIDO UNIQLO SAPPORO 7AKEN 2-2-1NISHI-KU2AKEN2JYO SAPPORO-SHI HOKKAIDO UNIQLO SAPPORO NAEBO 9-3-3BHIGASHI-KUHONCHI SAPPORO-SHI HOKKAIDO UNIQLO SAPPORO NAEBO 9-3-3BHIGASHI-KUHONCHI SAPPORO-SHI HOKKAIDO UNIQLO OTARU SUMIYOSHI OTARU HOKKAIDO UNIQLO ISHIKATIAYA-KAN 1-9-1 TARUKAWA1JYO HOKKAIDO UNIQLO FUJIRE CHITOSE EKI BUILDING3F 7-1789-2 CHIYODA-CHOH CHITOSE-SHI HOKKAIDO UNIQLO FURESUPOSHHIRONAKA 11-1NAKACHOHNAMIYOHNISHI OBIHIRO-SHI HOKKAIDO UNIQLO OBIHIRO 1-29-1 NISHI18JYOMINAMI OBIHIRO-SHI HOKKAIDO UNIQLO ABASHIRI 2-48-9TSUKISHIGAOKA ABASHIRI-SHI HOKKAIDO UNIQLO MUTSUTOMAOI TOMAKOMAI MALL-NAI 1-2-1KARANAKACHOH MUTSU-SHI AOMORI UNIQLO GOSHOGAWARA EL-MINOMACHI ELMINOMACHI SHOPPING CENTER-NAI 517-1KARAAKASAYANAGI FUJIMAKI HIROSAKI-SHI 3-1-30AZAWASEDA HIROSAKI-SHI AOMORI UNIQLO TOWADA 22DAZA 20AZACHUOHNISHI TOWADA-SHI AOMORI UNIQLO GARATONNNISHI8JYO-NAI MAEDA 2-3-11N6YOSHI AOMORI-SHI AOMORI UNIQLO HILASHIAOMORI 2-4-1HAMADATE AOMORI-SHI AOMORI UNIQLO HACHINOHE RAPIA 3FRAPIA MINNAMIAOBA-SHI AOMORI UNIQLO HACHINOHENIHINMATO1KADA 40-11AMBON-YANAGI MORIOKA2-SHI IWATE UNIQLO ICHINOHE 12-14-1KOYO HACHINOHE-SHI AOMORI UNIQLO HACHINOHENIHINMATO1KADA 40-11AMBON-YANAGI MORIOKA2-SHI IWATE UNIQLO ICHINOHE MI PLAZA 71-1BARTACHO KITAKAMI-SHI IWATE UNIQLO MFUPARIGARDEN 49-1 BIFU RIFU-CHO MIYAGI-GUN MIYAGI UNIQLO OGANARA 13BAZA KANAKO OGANARA-MACHI SHIBATA-GUN MIYAGI UNIQLO ISHINOMAKIHEBITA 895-1ABUTA AZA ISHINOMAKI-SHI MIYAGI UNIQLO ACROSSPLAZASAINAICHI 11-1SHIMEZAKU MIYAGINO-KU SENDAI-SHI MIYAGI UNIQLO YORKTOWNIZUMIOSAKI 2-14-1KOYO HACHINOHE-SHI AOMORI UNIQLO ICHINOMA 3F MIYAGI UNIQLO AZABATASHIHARAI A1AZAYASHIKI IZAI WAKABAYASHI-KU SENDAI-SHI MIYAGI UNIQLO GENDAIAEKI 3FAEKI 3-1CHUO AOBA-KU SENDAI-SHI MIYAGI UNIQLO NAIZAMINAMIINARABI 1-1AZAFUKUMUROHSOH DOMOKA TAIHAKU-KU SENDAI-SHI MIYAGI UNIQLO MINAMIYOSHINARITOWNPLAZA MINAMI 1-2MINNAMIYOSHINARIAOBA-KU SENDAI-SHI MIYAGI UNIQLO NATORI-SHI MIYAGI UNIQLO FURUKAWANAMI-NAI FURUKAWANAMIAMI TOCHIKUAKUSEIRUGTOUCHI 43GANU 4BANCHI MIYAGI FURUKAWANAMI-NAI FURUKAWANAMIAMI TOCHIKUAKUSEIRUGTOUCHI 43GANU 4BANCHI SANUMA 2-12-5AZA...HASAMACHOSANUMA TOME-SHI MIYAGI UNIQLO NATORI 8F-1TANOBE UEMATSU NATORI-SHI MIYAGI UNIQLO FURECUHOYONOTE FRIENDLY SPOTIKATE-NAI 185AZANAKAKASA YOKOTE-SHI UNIQLO AEON AKITANAKASAN 2FAEON AKITANAKASAN 1-1-1GOSHONOJIZODEN AKITA-SHI UNIQLO AKITA AEON AKITANAKASAN SHOPPINGCENTERUGTOUCHI 1-1ABASEDAADOHIGGAEN AKITA-SHI AKITA UNIQLO ODATENSHI ROCKTOWNODATENISHI-NAI 18-80NEGETOSHIMMACHI ODATE-SHI AKITA UNIQLO AKITA AOCHOHOSHOINDO SHOPPINGTOWN ACROSSHOSHIRO 80AZATERAMACHI NOSHIRO-SHI AKITA UNIQLO FURESUPOHONJJ 162SHINNARAIZA YURHOKU AKITA UNIQLO ZAONARISAWA 1-2-8NARISAWANISHI YAMAGATA UNIQLO YAMAGATA 1-2-1 TSURUKAWA YAMAGATA-SHI YAMAGATA UNIQLO TEPPO-MACHI YAMAGATA-SHI AGATA UNIQLO MAMEGASAKI 1-2-1MAMEGASAKI 3F YAMAGATA UNIQLO SHIN-AJ 128e-8TSUKACHIMACHI AZASHIMIZUGAWA SINJO-SHI AGATA UNIQLO WESTMALLPAL WESTMALLPALSC-NAI 3-15MISAKI-MACHI TSURUOKA-SHI YAMAGATA UNIQLO HOLOSHINE IPPONGITOCHIKUKAUGSEIR NAIAZGAKU3 2 HIGASHINE-SHI YAMAGATA UNIQLO AEONHIKAWA 2FAEONMIKAWASHOPPINGCENTERSENMONTENGAI 128-1WADAKONKOMIKAWA-MACHI HIGASHITAGAWA-GUN YAMAGATA UNIQLO YONEZAWA 16TOKIMACHI YONEZAWA-SHI YAMAGATA UNIQLO INAKOHARAKWA 32-1ONAHAMAOKAONAZA-XI IWAKI-SHI FUKUSHIMA UNIQLO IWARITAIRA 17TAIRAYAGAWASEAZAIZUMIMACHI IWAKI-SHI FUKUSHIMA UNIQLO AIZUWAKAMATU 2 YONEDAI AIZUWAKAMATSU-SHI FUKUSHIMA UNIQLO KORYIAMATOTSUKI 8BOTSUKIMACHIAZA KORIYAMA-SHI FUKUSHIMA UNIQLO YORKTOWN-NAI 12-13KKUTAMACHI KORIYAMA-SHI FUKUSHIMA UNIQLO ROCKTOWNKAGURAHAMA 11AZANAKAKOMACHI SUKAGAWA-SHI FUKUSHIMA UNIQLO HARAMACHI BIAFUREUSNO-NAI 26THARAMACHIKUMITAHIRAAZA MINAMISOMA-SHI FUKUSHIMA UNIQLO MEGASTAGESHIRAKAWA MEGASTAGESHIRAKAWA SC 26-1 TAKATAWA SIIRAKAWA-SHI FUKUSHIMA UNIQLO FUKUSHIMA KAMATA 23-1 KAMATA KUMAMOMAE FUKUSHIMA-SHI FUKUSHIMA UNIQLO FUKUSHIMA MAINNUAMSAWAMATA 83 YASHIMADA BIWAFUCHI FUKUSHIMA-SHI FUKUSHIMA UNIQLO LALA GARDEN TSUKUBA 27B-1ONIIZANISHENNGAGAI TSUK SHI IBARAKI UNIQLO REPUSA MALL 380-5 SHIMOHARA IEKMUKAI TSUKUBA-SHI IBARAKI UNIQLO HITACHINAKA NEWPORT 35-1 UHINKICHO HITACHI NAKA UNIQLO SUPER MALL 2219-8 SHIMICHEM INAIZUMI KOGA-SHI IBARAKI UNIQLO TUCHIURA 40A ARAKAWA TAKAHAGH-SHI IBARAKI UNIQLO TORIDE 3 TERADA ENDOUMAE TORIDE-SHI IBARAKI UNIQLO ACROSS MALL MORIYA 4-4-7 MATSUGAOKA MORIYA-SHI IBARAKI UNIQLO KASHIWA KAMEYJ 2 HORIWARI KAMEU-SHI IBARAKI UNIQLO MITOEKAIZKA 3-60-1 KEYAKIDAI MITO-SHI IBARAKI UNIQLO MITOMIWA 3-663-4 MIWA MITO-SHI IBARAKI UNIQLO TAKEKADE 1001-14 TAMADO CHIKUSEI-SHI IBARAKI UNIQLO TUCHIURA IWARAKI 3-5-3 MANAEBECYO TUCHIURA-SHI IBARAKI UNIQLO TSUCHIURA 2650-1 SUNN NAKA-SHI IBARAKI UNIQLO HITACHINARUSAWA 2-37-1ZNAKANARUSAWACYO HITACHI-SHI IBARAKI UNIQLO RYUGASAKI NEWTOWN 1-1-1FUJINAMA RYUGASAKI-SHI IBARAKI UNIQLO UTE 2-26-1 UNGSATO HARAGAWA TOCHIGI UNIQLO UTSUNOMIYA 4-2-1 YOTO UTSUNOMIYA-SHI UTSUNOMIYAHOSOTTANI 311 HOSOTANICYO UTSUNOMIYA-SHI TOCHIGI UNIQLO UTSUNOMIYA18URUTA 3493-1 TSURUTACYO UTSUNOMIYA TO UNIQLO IMAIZUMI 1615 IMAIZUMICHO UTSUNOMIYA TOCHIGI UNIQLO ISHIBASHI 2952-3 SHIMOKOYAMA SHIMONO-SHI TOCHIGI UNIQLO IANO 32 CHO SANO-SHI TOCHIGI UNIQLO OYAMA 24-48 NISHISUTONAN OYAMA-SHI TOCHIGI UNIQLO MOIKA 3-5-1 KAMKKOMAGI MOOKA-SHI TOCHIGI UNIQ ASHIKAGA 1-243-8 ASAKURACHO ASHIKAGA-SHI TOCHIGI UNIQLO OHTAWARA 1-6-44 MIHARA OHTAWARA-SHI TOCHIGI UNIQLO KATSANAGOCHO TOCHIGI-SHI TOCHIGI UNIQLO MAICHI 46-1 TOYOTA NIKKOU-SHI TOCHIGI UNIQLO FUJINAKA 2A60-1 IWAI ANNAKA-SHI GUNMA UNIQLO KI 3093-17 TSUNATORIMACHI ISEZAKI-SHI GUNMA UNIQLO 1099-1 FUJINAKACHO FUJIHARABAE TATEBAYASHI-SHI GUNMA UNIQLO KETTOTY 1-12A-1 AICHCHO KIRYU-SHI GUNMA UNIQLO TAKASAKIHIKACYO 182-1 SHINNOKUTOMACHI TAKASAKI-SHI GUNMA UNIQLO TAKASAMTOB MAICH 2-11-9 TONYAMACHI TAKASAKI-SHI GUNMA UNIQLO 143-1 ABRA ASHIDA SHIBUKAWA-SHI GUNMA UNIQLO MAEBASHINAGAH 247-1 SEKINECYO MAEBASHI-SHI GUNMA UNIQLO MAEBASHISHI 89-1 SOLIYAMI UEHARACHO NUMATA-SHI GUNMA UNIQLO MAEBASHIGOMEN 247-1 SEKINECYO MAEBASHI-SHI GUNMA UNIQLO MAEBASHISHI 89-1 SOLIYAMI TAKAI JYURO BAEBASHI-SHI GUNMA UNIQLO AMAKAWASHIIMA 1-2-1 AMAKAWAGHIHMACHI MAEBASHI-SHI GUNMA UNIQLO OHTA 324-1 ARAI OHTA-SHI GUNMA UNIQLO FUJIKA 165 SHINKURISU FUJIOKA-SHI GUNMA UNIQLO TOMIOKA 1000-1 TOMIOKA KITAHATA TOMIOKA-SHI GUNMA UNIQLO AEON URANGAMIGNOS 2710 MIDORIKUSHAZA DAMON SAITAMA-SHI UNIQLO ITOYOKADO OHMIYA MIYAHATA 1-1-1 KITAKU MIYAHARACHO SAITAMA-SHI MA-SHI SAITAMA UNIQLO LUMINE OHMIYA LLMINEDAPT 63D OHMIYAKUNISHKICHO SAITAMA-SHI SAITAMA UNIQLO URANGATAKUBO 1697-1 MIKA DAITAKUBO SAITAMA-SHI SAITAMA UNIQLO OHMIYA DHWADA 1-116P-1 MINUMAKU OHWADACHO SAITAMA-SHI SAITAMA UNIQLO ITOYOKADO SAITA NISHIKU UCHINHOHNOO SAITAMA-SHI UNIQLO KONN 4-16-3 CHUUSHI HONCHO NISHI SAITAMA-SHI UNIQLO KOSHIGAYA 174-7 DAI KOSHIGAYA-SHI SAITAMA UNIQLO MINNAMIKOSHIGAYA OPN OPASF 1-15-1 MINNAMIKOSHIGAYA KOSHIGAYA-SHI SAITAMA UNIQLO KUKI 871-19 KOGURI KAA KUKI-SHI SAITAMA UNIQLO CALFOOL SAITAMA SHOPPINGMALL 1F 1126-1 KAMOGAWA KUMAGAYA 2-1-45 TSUKICHO KUMAGAYA-SHI SAIT

A.

B.

アートマガジン ／ ART MAGAZINE

WERK MAGAZINE ［アートマガジン］
WERK MAGAZINE ［Art magazine］
CD, D: THESEUS CHAN
AD: MARINA LIM
DF, SB: WORK

A. 乾燥させた新聞用紙を使用して本文用紙をささくれ立たせ、表紙はスプレーでペインとして仕上げた。
Utilizing dried newsprint paper, the inside pages are rough and abraded. The cover has been spray painted.

B. 表紙を手作業のパッチワークで仕上げ、乾燥させた新聞用紙を使用し、本文用紙をささくれ立たせている。
Utilizing dried newsprint paper, the inside pages are rough and abraded. The covers feature handmade patchwork collages.

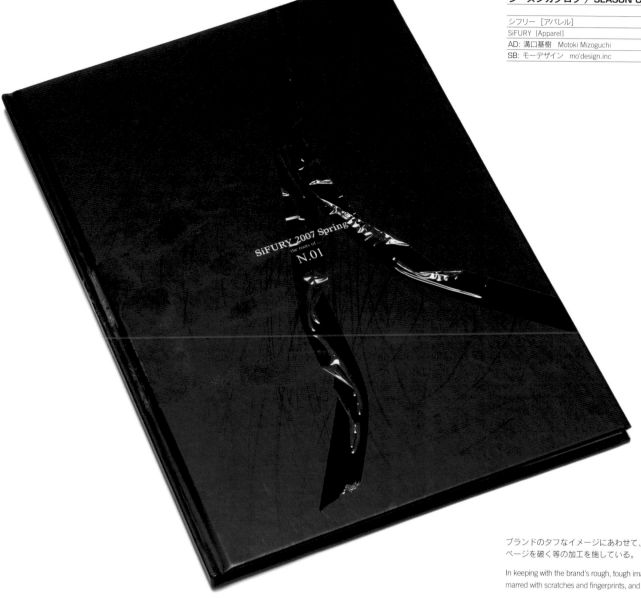

シーズンカタログ／SEASON CATALOGUE

シフリー ［アパレル］

SiFURY ［Apparel］

AD: 溝口基樹　Motoki Mizoguchi

SB: モーデザイン　mo'design.inc

ブランドのタフなイメージにあわせて、表紙に指紋をつけたり、
ページを破く等の加工を施している。

In keeping with the brand's rough, tough image, the cover appears to be
marred with scratches and fingerprints, and the pages crumpled and torn.

シーズンカタログ / SEASON CATALOGUE

ステューシージャパン ［アパレル］
STUSSY JAPAN ［Apparel］
AD: 溝口基樹　MOTOKI MIZOGUCHI
SB: モーデザイン　mo'design.inc

モーテル ［アパレル］
MOTEL [Apparel]
CD, AD, D: NESCO　NESCO
P: 清水将之(es-quisse)　Masayuki Shimizu (es-quisse)
DF: NIGREC DESIGN　NIGREC DESIGN
SB: モーテル　MOTEL

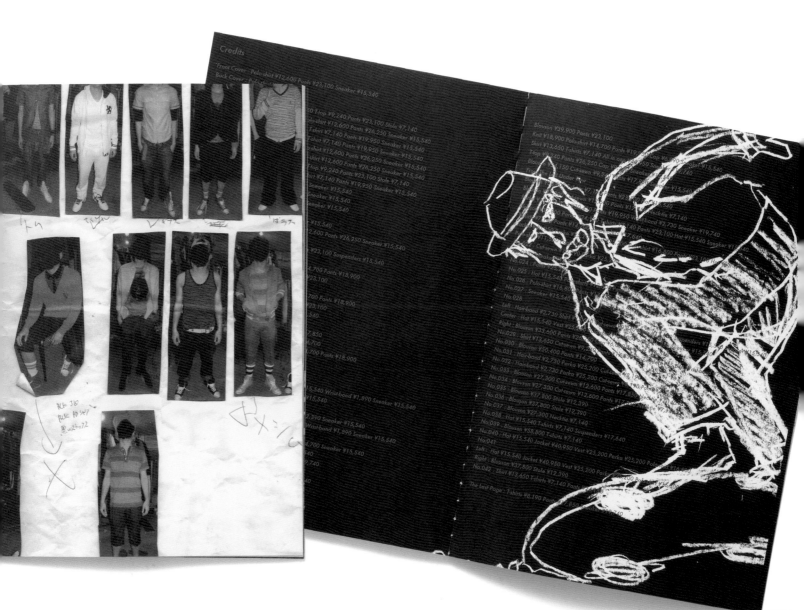

ラッピングペーパー (Spiral Online Store) /
WRAPPING PAPER

スパイラル [複合文化施設]
Spiral [Complex culture facility]
AD, D, SB: グルーヴィジョンズ　groovisions

フリーペーパー / **FREE PAPER**

エム・ティーヴィー・ジャパン [音楽エンタテインメントテレビチャンネル]
MTV JAPAN [Music entertainment TVchannel]
AD, D, SB: グルーヴィジョンズ　groovisions

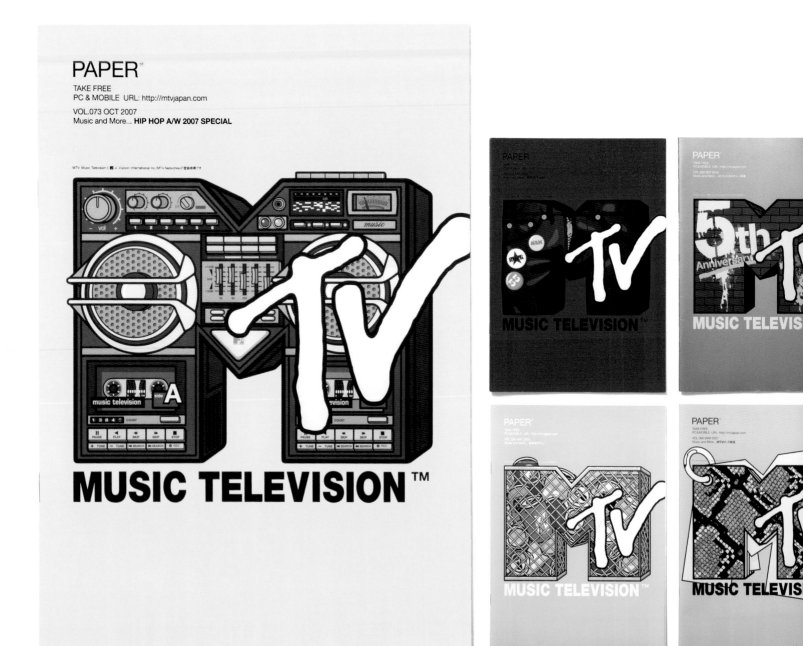

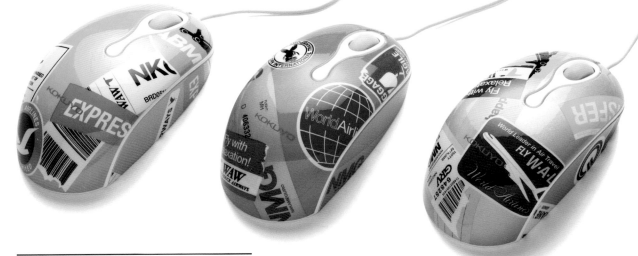

マウス(100周年PC用バラエティセットより) / MOUSE

コクヨS&T [文具メーカー]
KOKUYO S&T CO.,Ltd. [Stationery maker]
AD, D, SB: グルーヴィジョンズ groovisions

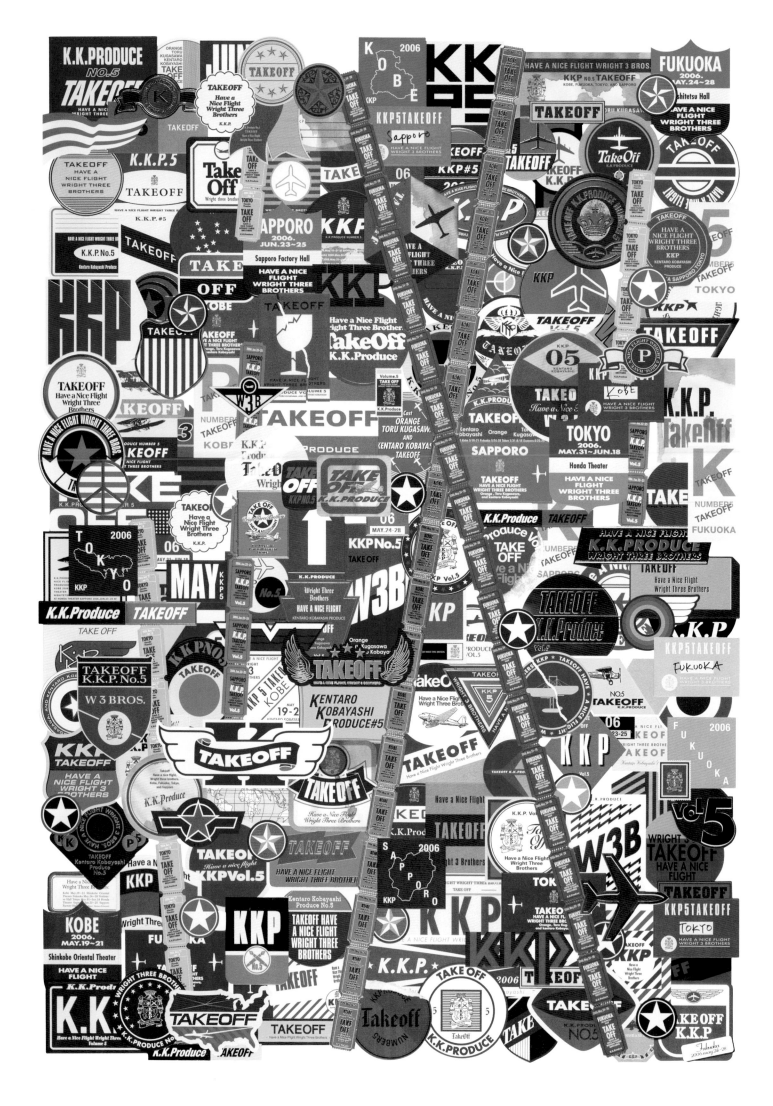

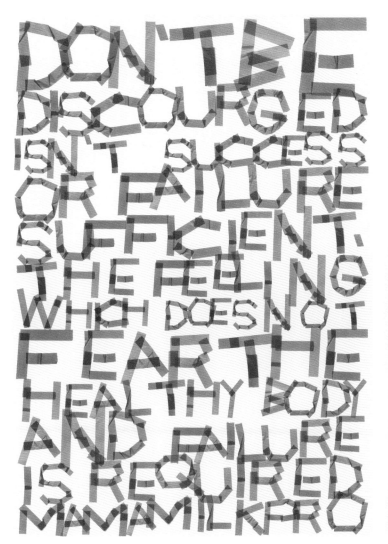

公演案内ポスター ／
PERFORMANCE INFORMATION POSTER

ママミルクプロ ［劇団］
MAMA-MILK.PRO [Theatrical company]
CD, AD, D, SB: 小杉幸一　Koichi Kosugi

年賀状 / NEW YEAR CARD

コミューングラフィックス ［デザイン事務所］
COMMUNE GRAPHICS [Design Office]
AD, D: 上田 亮　Ryo Ueda
DF, SB: コミューングラフィックス　COMMUNE GRAPHICS

POSTCARD

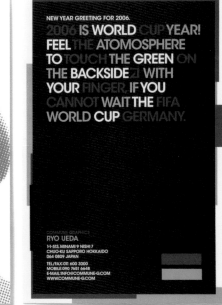

NEW YEAR GREETING FOR 2006.
2006 IS WORLD CUP YEAR!
FEEL THE ATOMOSPHERE
TO TOUCH THE GREEN ON
THE BACKSIDE ZI WITH
YOUR FINGER. IF YOU
CANNOT WAIT THE FIFA
WORLD CUP GERMANY.

COMMUNE GRAPHICS
RYO UEDA
11-513, MINAMI 9 NISHI 7
CHUO-KU SAPPORO HOKKAIDO
064 0809 JAPAN
TEL/FAX 011 600 3000
MOBILE 090 7651 6648
E-MAIL INFO@COMMUNE-G.COM
WWW.COMMUNE-G.COM

公演案内ポスター ／
PERFORMANCE INFORMATION POSTER

トゥインクルコーポレーション ［劇団］
TWINKLE Corporation Ltd. [Theater]
CD, AD: 水野 学　Manabu Mizuno
D: 上村 昌　Masaru Uemura / 仲山慎哉　Shinya Nakayama
DF, SB: グッドデザインカンパニー　good design company co., ltd.

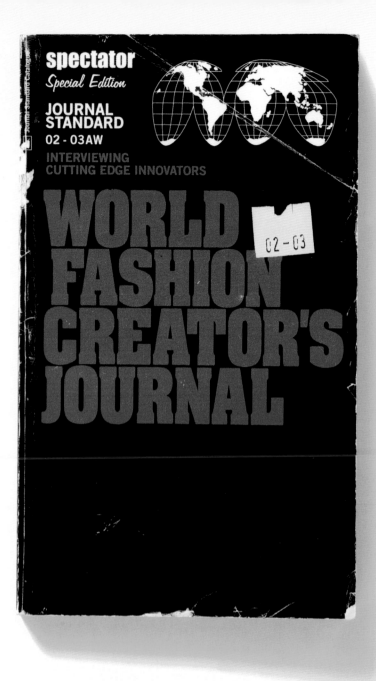

PARIS

LONDON

NEW YORK

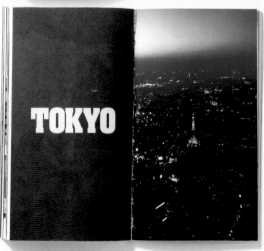

TOKYO

シーズンカタログ / SEASON CATALOG

ジャーナルスタンダード ［アパレル］
JOURNAL STANDARD [Apparel]
CD: 青野利光　Toshimitsu Aono
D, DF: 峯崎ノリテル　Noriteru Minezaki
SB: スタジオ　(STUDIO)

「旅行」というシーズンコンセプトにあわせて、折れ痕や擦れたよ
うな加工を施し「旅行に持参して古びた」ように仕上げている。

In keeping with the season's concept of "travel," the booklet has
been invested with folds and rub marks to create the kind of wear-
and-tear associated with travel.

KK OUTLET

YOU ARE:			ON:		
INVITED	●		SATURDAY JUNE 14th 2008 9.00PM		
PROVOKED			FRIDAY FEBRUARY 1st 2008 7.00PM	●	
SCARED			FRIDAY DECEMBER 25th 2009 5.00AM		
DISGUSTED			FRIDAY JANUARY 1st 2010 1.00AM		

TO ATTEND:			FOR:		
A SERVICE STATION			MASSAGE		
KK OUTLET	●		DUTCH LESSONS		
THE LAUNDROMAT			DRINKS	●	
HARDWARE SHOP			BURLESQUE DANCING		

AT:			BECAUSE:		
42 HOXTON SQUARE	●		YOU OWE US MONEY		
12 WHITES ROW			YOUR HAIR SMELLS NICE		
LAURIERGRACHT 39			IT'S OUR OPENING	●	
41 WHITCOMB STREET			YOU'VE GOT THE KEYS		

rsvp@kkoutlet.com KesselsKramer London 42 Hoxton Square London N1 6PB Tel +44 (0)207 033 7680 www.kkoutlet.com

オープニングパーティー案内状 /
OPENING PARTY INVITATION

KK OUTLET ［エージェンシー＆ショップ＆ギャラリー］
KK OUTLET ［Communication agency & Shop & Gallery］
CD, AD: Erik Kessels
CW: Dave Beil
I: Anthony Bueeill
DF, SB: Kessels Kramer

270/297/324/352/446GSM

紙見本 / PAPER SWATCH

平和紙業(香港)有限公司　[紙卸商]
Heiwa Paper Hong Kong　[Paper Merchant]
AD: Eddy Yu / Hung Lam
D: PakSum Leung
I: Computerhead
DF, SB: CoDesign Ltd.

展示会インビテーション、カタログ／
SHOW INVITATION, CATALOGUE

コンバースフットウェア［シューズメーカー］
CONVERSE FOOTWEAR CO.,LTD [Shoes maker]
CD, PL: 勢井浩二郎　Kojiro Sei
AD: 本村耕平　Kohei Motomura
D: 村井保介　Yasusuke Murai
CW: 山本雅治　Masaharu Yamamoto
DF, SB: デキスギ　DEKISUGI CORPORATION

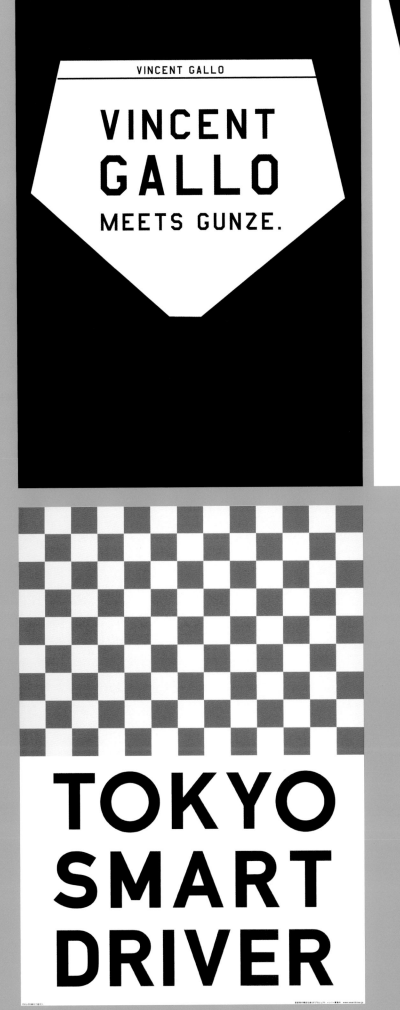

VINCENT GALLO

VINCENT
GALLO
MEETS GUNZE.

TOKYO
SMART
DRIVER

展覧会ポスター / EXHIBITION POSTER

博報堂 [広告代理店]
HAKUHODO INC. [Advertising agency]
CD: 嶋 浩一郎 Koichiro Shima
AD: 佐野研二郎 Kenjiro Sano
D: 小杉幸一 Koichi Kosugi / 岡本和樹 Kazuki Okamoto /
　　長嶋りかこ Rikako Nagashima
SB: 博報堂 HAKUHODO Inc. MR_DESIGN MR_DESIGN

キャンペーンポスター /CAMPAIGN POSTER

首都高速道路 [道路公団]
Metropolitan Expressway Co.,ltd. [Highway Public Corporation]
CD: 小山薫堂 Kundo Koyama / 嶋浩一郎 Koichiro Shima
AD: 水野 学 Manabu Mizuno
D: 上村 昌 Masaru Uemura / 古屋貴広 Takahiro Furuya
CW: 小薬 元 Gen Kogusuri
PLANNER: 萩尾友樹 Tomoki Hagio / 森川 俊 Syun Morikawa
PR: 山名清隆 Kiyotaka Yamana / 軽部政治 Seiji Karube
DF, SB: グッドデザインカンパニー good design company co., ltd.

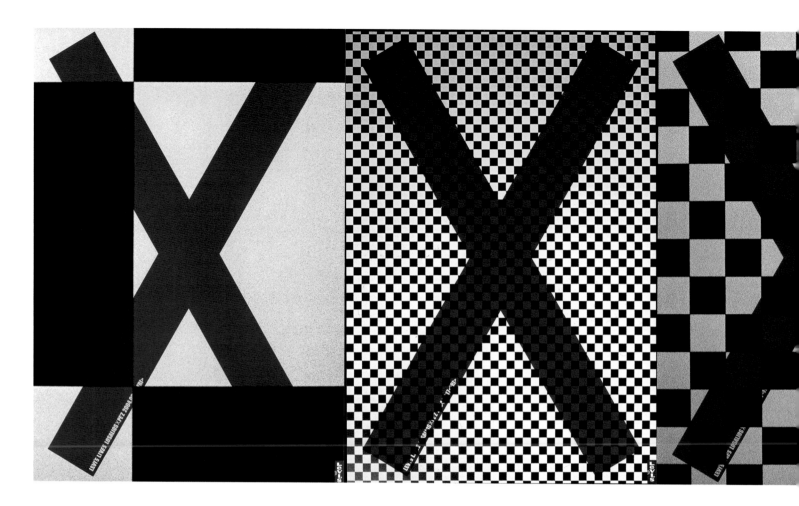

イベント告知ポスター /
EVENT ANNOUNCEMENT POSTER

リーバイス・ストラウスジャパン ［アパレル］
Levi Strauss Japan K.K. [Apparel]
AD, CD, CW: 山本武志　Takeshi Yamamoto
AD, D, CW: 青木二郎　Jiro Aoki
SB: アサツー ディ・ケイ　ASATSU-DK INC.

アートマガジン / ART MAGAZINE

WERK MAGAZINE ［アートマガジン］
WERK MAGAZINE [Art magazine]
CD, D: THESEUS CHAN
AD: MARINA LIM
DF, SB: WORK

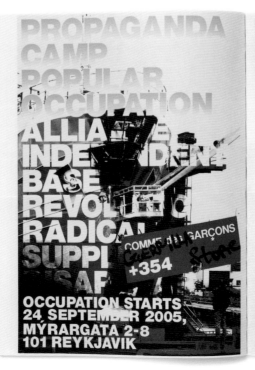

Guerrilla Store +354

DISAPPEARED
Mýrargata 2-8, 101 Reykjavik, Iceland
24 September 2005 – 25 September 2006
GS is installed in a former metal factory in the
dry dock of the city's harbour. Palettes and found
furniture serve as part of the display furniture.

ブランドポスター / BRANDING POSTER

ナイキジャパン [アパレル]
NIKE JAPAN [Apparel]
CD: 米村 浩　Hiroshi Yonemura
AD: ジーノ・ウー　Gino Woo
D: 富山庄太郎　Shotaro Tomiyama
CW: 門井隆盛　Takamori Kadoi
ART BUYER: 飯田昭雄　Akio Iida
ACCOUNT: アンソニー松尾　Anthony Matsuo
SB: ワイデン＋ケネディ トウキョウ　Wieden + Kennedy Tokyo

フリーペーパー / FREE PAPER

ナイキジャパン ［アパレル］
NIKE JAPAN ［Apparel］
CD: 米村 浩　Hiroshi Yonemura
AD: ジーノ・ウー　Gino Woo
D: 富山庄太郎　Shotaro Tomiyama
CW: 門井隆盛　Takamori Kadoi / 尚師喜和子　Kiwako Takashi
ART BUYER: 飯田昭雄　Akio Iida
ACCOUNT: 足立公平　Kohei Adachi
SB: ワイデン＋ケネディ トウキョウ　Wieden + Kennedy Tokyo

フリーペーパー / FREE PAPER

ナイキジャパン ［アパレル］
NIKE JAPAN ［Apparel］
CD: 米村 浩　Hiroshi Yonemura
AD: ジーノ・ウー　Gino Woo
D: 富山庄太郎　Shotaro Tomiyama
CW: 岩井俊介　Shunsuke Iwai / 尚師喜和子　Kiwako Takashi
ART BUYER: 飯田昭雄　Akio Iida
ACCOUNT: シグ セング　Shig Seng
SB: ワイデン＋ケネディ トウキョウ　Wieden + Kennedy Tokyo

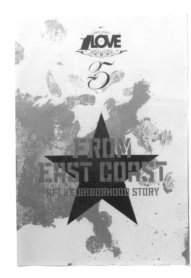

フリーペーパー / FREE PAPER

KDDI ［電気通信事業］
KDDI CORPORATION ［Telecommunications business］
CD, AD: 日高英輝　Eiki Hidaka
D: 竹林一茂　Kazushige Takebayashi / 河上 聡　Satoshi Kawakami
CW: 小川英紀　Hidenori Ogawa
P: TAKA　TAKA
DF, SB: グリッツデザイン　gritzdesign inc.

キャンペーン用ブックカバー ／
BOOK COVER FOR CAMPAIGN

集英社 ［出版社］
SHUEISHA ［Publisher］
AD, D: 長井健太郎　Kentaro Nagai
CW: © LUCKY LAND COMMUNICATIONS/SHUEISHA
DF, SB: グラフレックスディレクションズ　Graflex Directions

展覧会案内ポスター、カタログ /
EXHIBITION ANNOUNCEMENT POSTER,
CATALOGUE

日本科学未来館 [施設]
Miraikan [Facility]
AD, DF, SB: 氏デザイン　ujidesign

ポスター、CDパッケージ / POSTER, CD

ユニバーサルミュージック ［音楽制作事業］
UNIVERSAL MUSIC K.K. ［Music contents production］
CD: グーフィ森　Goofy Mori / 大西智恵　Chie Onishi
AD, D: 青木克憲　Katsunori Aoki
D: 高桑佳奈　Kana Takakuwa
I: 寄藤文平　Bunpei Yorifuji
DF, SB: バタフライ・ストローク　butterfly stroke inc.

CD

Yeah!Yeah!Yeah!Records ［音楽レーベル］
Yeah!Yeah!Yeah!Records ［Music label］
AD, D, SB: グルーヴィジョンズ　groovisions

今日、世界に最も誇れる日本は何だ。富士山の美しさか。たゆまぬ勤勉さか。メジャーのマウンドに立つ若き大投手か。いずれもそう言えるだろう。しかし、ひとつ忘れてはいないか。ハリウッドの巨匠から路地裏を駆ける子どもたちまで、世界中の人々を驚嘆し、熱狂し、愛してやまない日本がある。それは、ANIMEだ。2007年夏。ANIMEは再び、世界を驚かすことになる。スタジオ4℃の名の下に、現在のジャパニーズ・アニメーションで考えうる最強の才能たちが集結。前代未聞のオムニバスムービーを作り上げた。無限に広がる想像力のキャンバスを躍動する、大胆かつ繊細な映像テクニック。そして、息をもつかせぬストーリー展開。7人の映像作家の個性は、ときに対峙し、ときに共鳴しながら見る者の感性を直撃する。Genius Party—この作品こそ今日、世界に最も誇れる日本だ。

What's the pride of Japa
diligence? How about a
your time, there are no wr
inspires awe and madnes
titans to street kids. We'
world again. Talent once
an unprecedented film co
with the most powerful ta
industry. Limitless creativ
sensitive cinematic tricks
of seven auteurs-sometim
jugular of the senses. Le

Genius Party™

STUDIO4℃ Presents / 7 IMPACTS by 7 DIRECTORS / www.genius-party.jp

What's the pride of Japan today?
Is it the beauty of Mt. Fuji? Maybe our sense of diligence?
How about a young pitcher standing on a Major-League mound?
Take your time, there are no wrong answers.
But we hope you're not missing one.
HINT: It inspires awe and madness and love in people around the world, from Holly
We're talking about ANIME. And in July 2007, it will rock the world again.
Talent once divided has united beneath the STUDIO4℃ flag to call them.
The list of creators was built up to call them.
who with the most powerful talents and recognized as the top in the Japanese anim
Limitless creativity dancing across the canvas in illustrations both bold and sensiti
and stories that leave no time to breathe.
The personalities of seven auteurs-sometimes facing off,
sometimes resonating, always going for the jugular of the senses.
Let's face it: Genius Party. This is the pride of Japan today.

Genius Party™

STUDIO4℃ Presents / 7 IMPACTS by 7 DIRECTORS / www.genius-party.jp

Gen

WHAT
GENI
PAR

STUDIO4℃

THIS PROJECT IS PRODUCED BY STUDIO4℃

プレスシート、パンフレット /
PRESS SHEET, BROCHURE

スタジオ4℃ ［映画］	
STUDIO4℃ ［Movie］	
CD: 山下信一	Shinichi Yamashita
AD, D: 野尻大作	Daisaku Nojiri
D: 戸崎正浩	Masahiro Tozaki / 安達明日香 Asuka Adachi
DF, SB: ground	ground

t the beauty of Mt. Fuji? Maybe our sense of
r standing on a Major-League mound? Take
. But we hope you're not missing one. HINT: It
in people around the world, from Hollywood
out ANIME. And in July 2007, it will rock the
united beneath the STUDIO4℃ flag to create
list of creators was built up to call them, who
cognized as the top in the Japanese animation
across the canvas in illustrations both bold and
hat leave no time to breathe. The personalities
f, sometimes resonating, always going for the
Genius Party. This is the pride of Japan today.

Genius Party™

STUDIO4℃ Presents / 7 IMPACTS by 7 DIRECTORS / www.genius-party.jp

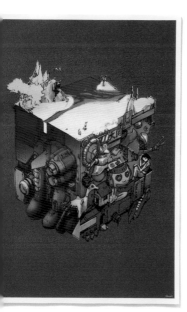

What's the pride of Japan today?
Is it the beauty of Mt. Fuji? Maybe our sense of diligence?
How about a young pitcher standing on a Major-League mound?
Take your time, there are no wrong answers.
But we hope you're not missing one.
HINT: It inspires awe and madness and love in people around the world, from Holly
We're talking about ANIME. And in July 2007, it will rock the world again.
Talent once divided has united beneath the STUDIO4℃ flag to create an unprecede
The list of creators was built up to call them,
who with the most powerful talents and recognized as the top in the Japanese anim
Limitless creativity dancing across the canvas in illustrations both bold and sensiti
and stories that leave no time to breathe.
The personalities of seven auteurs-sometimes facing off,
sometimes resonating, always going for the jugular of the senses.
Let's face it: Genius Party. This is the pride of Japan today.

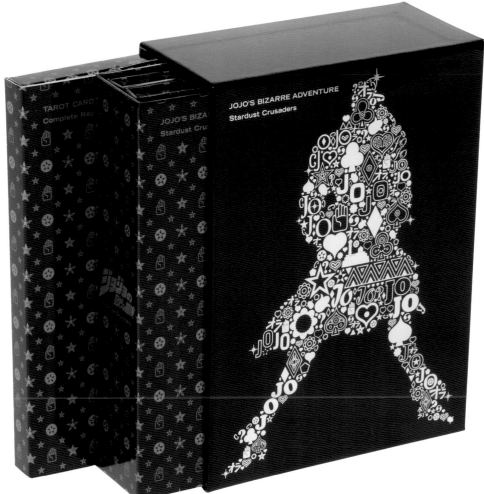

DVD-BOX

集英社＋クロックワークス ［出版社＋映像制作会社］
SHUEISHA + KLOCK WORX ［Publisher + Film corporation］
AD, D: 長井健太郎　Kentaro Nagai
COPY RIGHT: © Hirohiko Araki & LUCKY LAND
　　　　　　COMMUNICATIONS/SHUEISHA,A.P.P.P.
DF, SB: グラフレックスディレクションズ　Graflex Directions

CI計画書、ヘルメット /
CI PLANING BOOK, HELMET

ヨドプレ ［建築業］
YODO PLY CO. ［Architecture industry］
AD: 北川一成　Issay Kitagawa
DF, SB: グラフ　GRAPH CO.,LTD.

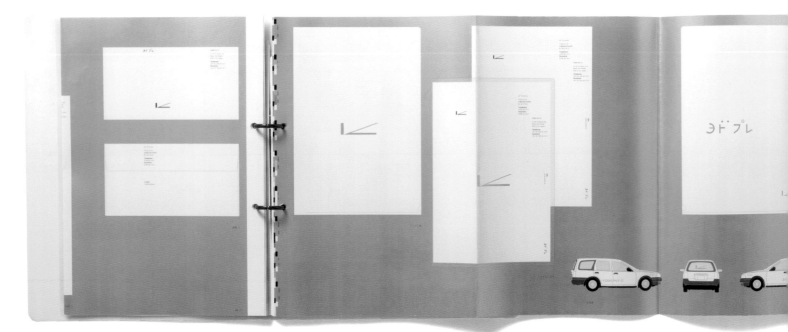

CHIC

Luxurious / Gracious / Mature
高級感のある / 落ち着いた / 大人な

Eiki Hidaka – a "tough" designer talks about "tough-style" design

The most important question when designing advertising is "What kind of product is it?" If the story behind the product and the concept is clear, the product will communicate itself. An example would be the advertising for Zero Halliburton that involved a standardized branding across the world. I constructed the look of the world brand with specs only, without catch copy. And by focusing in on the precision details, men - the target market - just melt (laughs). The methodology is the same for the design of corporate advertising. I think the ideal approach involves replacing the look of a company with an identity and then emphasizing whatever is unique about the company. Simply and directly conveying what the company stands for. It may just be that kind of stripped-back design that doesn't require endless discussion, that gives it a masculine feel.

The objective of black

I use black whenever I want to throw a light on the subject. Black is a color that makes the outline of objects stand out. The moment I use black, the subject is clear-cut. For me, black is the color you choose when you make to make a statement.

EIKI HIDAKA
Art director. Principal of Gritz Design
Born 1962 in Miyazaki. In 1989, he joined Draft and in 1998 was the recipient of a JAGDA New Designer Award. In 2000, he was awarded the International Poster Triennial Toyama Bronze Medal and in 2001, went out on his own, setting up Gritz Design. In the same year, he was awarded the New York ADC Silver and in 2004, the Nikkei Advertising Grand Prix. His art direction ranges from company branding, symbol marks and logotypes to package, product and book design.

His Works / P046-047, P100, P116-119, P120-121, P160

『男』なデザイナーの語る『男』なデザイン／日髙英輝

広告を設計する際に最も重要なのは「いかなる商品か」ということ。商品の歴史、コンセプトがきちんとしていれば、商品を登場させるだけで十分なコミュニケーションがとれます。たとえば世界共通のブランディングを手がけた「ゼロハリバートン」での表現がそう(P116-119)。世界ブランドという顔つきをキャッチコピーなし、スペックのみで構成しました。また精密な部品のアップにターゲットである男性は "しずる" んですよ（笑）。企業広告でも設計方法は同じ。企業の佇まいを人格に置き換え、その個性を際立たせることが最適な表現につながると考えています。シンプルに主義主張をまっすぐ伝える。そんな削ぎ落とした「四の五の言わない」表現が、男っぽいデザインと感じさせる理由かもしれません。

黒の目的

黒は存在をハッキリさせたいときに使います。黒は輪郭を際立たせる色。黒を使った瞬間にその対象は規定されると考えています。私にとって黒は、意思をハッキリ主張したいときに選択する色です。

日髙英輝
アートディレクター。グリッツデザイン代表。
1962年宮崎県生まれ。1989年ドラフト入社。1998年JAGDA新人賞受賞。2000年世界ポスタートリエンナーレトヤマ ブロンズアワード受賞。2001年独立し、グリッツデザインを設立。同年ニューヨークADC銀賞受賞。2004年日経広告賞グランプリ受賞。企業ブランディングからシンボル＆ロゴタイプ、パッケージ、グッズデザイン、装丁等のアートディレクションを行う。

作品掲載ページ／P46-47, P100, P116-119, P120-121, P160

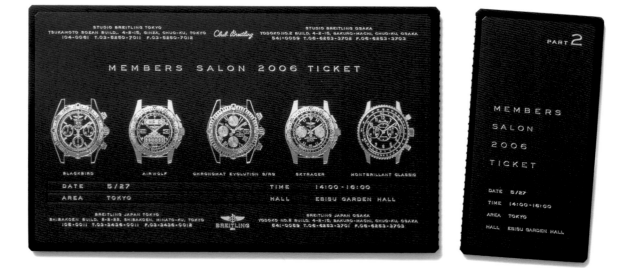

メンバーズサロンチケット 2006 /
MEMBERS SALON TICKET 2006

ブライトリング・ジャパン ［時計販売代理店］
BREITLING JAPAN LTD. ［Watch selling agent］
CD: 宮田 識　Satoru Miyata
CD, CW: 広瀬正明　Masaaki Hirose
AD: 古屋友章　Tomoaki Furuya
D: 平野篤史 /
DIGITAL ARTIST: 赤木康隆　Yasutaka Akagi
PR: 西面俊英　Toshihide Nishio
DF, SB: ドラフト　DRAFT Co.,Ltd.

卓上カレンダー 2008 /
DESK CALENDAR 2008

ブライトリング・ジャパン ［時計販売代理店］
BREITLING JAPAN LTD. ［Watch selling agent］
CD: 宮田 識　Satoru Miyata
CD, CW: 広瀬正明　Masaaki Hirose
AD: 古屋友章　Tomoaki Furuya
D: 平野篤史　Atsushi Hirano / 赤木康隆　Yasutaka Akagi
PR: 西面俊英　Toshihide Nishio
DF, SB: ドラフト　DRAFT Co.,Ltd.

展示会案内状 2005 / EXHIBITION INVITATION 2005

ブライトリング・ジャパン [時計販売代理店]	
BREITLING JAPAN LTD. [Watch selling agent]	
CD: 宮田 識	Satoru Miyata
CD, CW: 広瀬正明	Masaaki Hirose
AD, D: 古屋友章	Tomoaki Furuya
D: 平野篤史	Atsushi Hirano / 赤木康隆 Yasutaka Akagi
PR: 西面俊英	Toshihide Nishio
DF, SB: ドラフト	DRAFT Co.,Ltd.

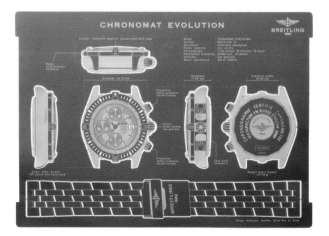

展示会案内状 2004 / EXHIBITION INVITATION 2004

ブライトリング・ジャパン［時計販売代理店］
BREITLING JAPAN LTD. [Watch selling agent]
CD: 宮田 識　Satoru Miyata
CD, CW: 広瀬正明　Masaaki Hirose
AD, D: 古屋友章　Tomoaki Furuya
PR: 西面俊英　Toshihide Nishio
DF, SB: ドラフト　DRAFT Co.,Ltd.

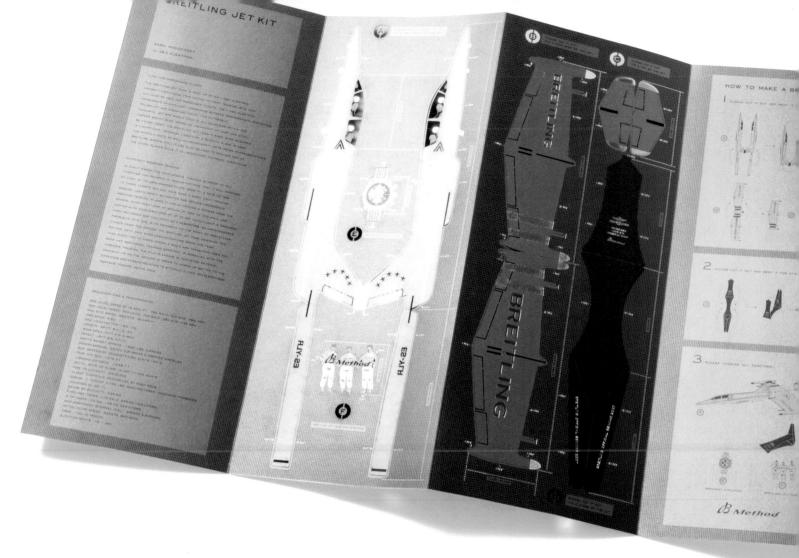

展示会案内状 2005 / EXHIBITION INVITATION 2005

ブライトリング・ジャパン [時計販売代理店]
BREITLING JAPAN LTD. [Watch selling agent]
CD: 宮田 識　Satoru Miyata
CD, CW: 広瀬正明　Masaaki Hirose
AD: 古屋友章　Tomoaki Furuya
PR: 西面俊秀　Toshihide Nishio
DF, SB: ドラフト　DRAFT Co.,Ltd.

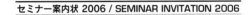

セミナー案内状 2007 / SEMINAR INVITATION 2007

ブライトリング・ジャパン [時計販売代理店]
BREITLING JAPAN LTD. [Watch selling agent]
CD: 宮田 識　Satoru Miyata
CD, CW: 広瀬正明　Masaaki Hirose
AD: 古屋友章　Tomoaki Furuya
D: 平野篤史　Atsushi Hirano
DIGITAL ARTIST: 赤木康隆　Yasutaka Akagi
DF, SB: ドラフト　DRAFT Co.,Ltd.

セミナー案内状 2006 / SEMINAR INVITATION 2006

ブライトリング・ジャパン [時計販売代理店]
BREITLING JAPAN LTD. [Watch selling agent]
CD: 宮田 識　Satoru Miyata
CD, CW: 広瀬正明　Masaaki Hirose
AD, P: 古屋友章　Tomoaki Furuya
D: 平野篤史　Atsushi Hirano
PR: 樋野晶子　Akiko Hino
DF, SB: ドラフト　DRAFT Co.,Ltd.

ZERO Polycarbonate / Frame / 21inch / gloss silver / ¥ 77,700

ブランド新聞広告 / BRANDING NEWSPAPER AD

エース［カバン製造販売］
ACE Co.,Ltd. ［Bag Manufacture&Sales］
CD, AD: 日高英輝　Eiki Hidaka
D: 相田俊一　Shunichi Aita / 竹林一茂　Kazushige Takebayashi
P: 数井啓介　Keisuke Kazui
CW: 渡辺潤平　Junpei Watanabe
DF, SB: グリッツデザイン　gritzdesign inc.

ZERO Polycarbonate / Frame / 26inch / mat silver / ¥ 89,250

ZERO Polycarbonate / Frame / 24inch / mat silver / ¥ 84,000

ZERO polycarbonate

ショップオープニング案内状、ノベルティ(キャラメル)、タグ、カタログ /
SHOP OPENING INVITATION, NOVELTY (CARAMEL), TAG, CATALOGUE

エース [カバン製造販売]
ACE Co.,Ltd. [Bag Manufacture&Sales]
CD, AD: 日高英輝　Eiki Hidaka
D: 相田俊一　Shunichi Aita / 竹林一茂　Kazushige Takebayashi
P: 数井啓介　Keisuke Kazui
C: 渡辺潤平　Junpei Watanabe
DF, SB: グリッツデザイン　gritzdesign inc

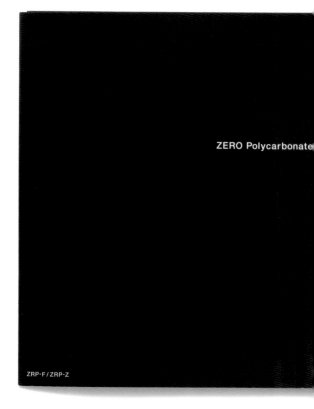

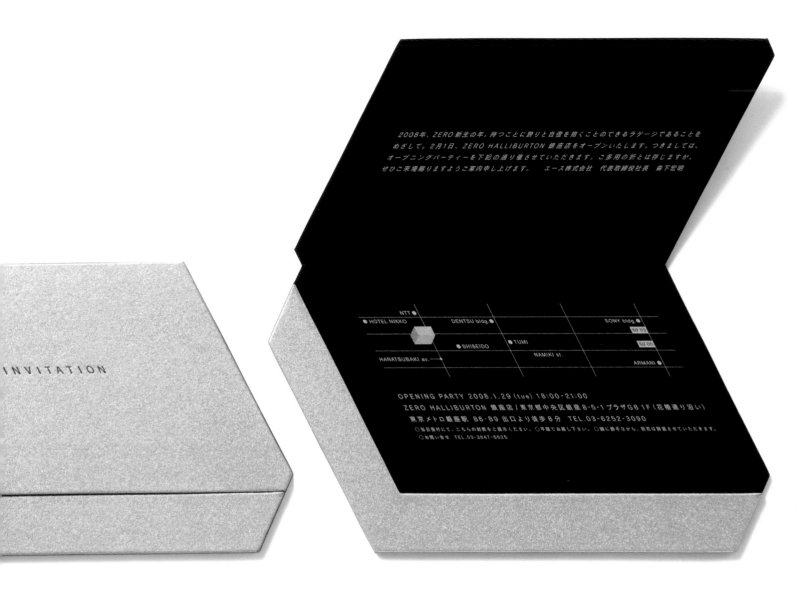

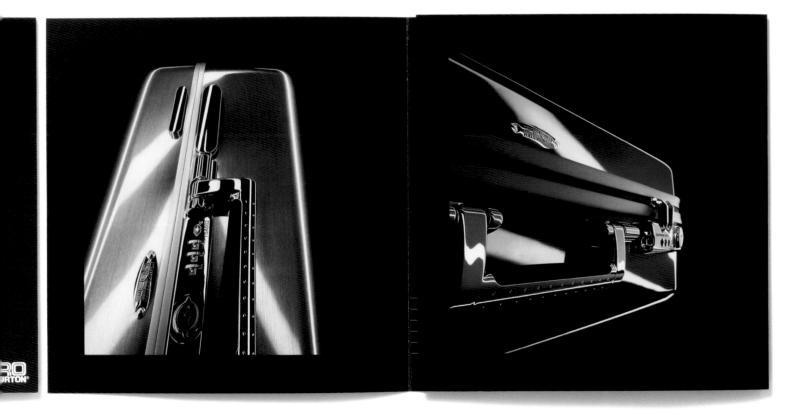

広州トヨタ自動車 [自動車メーカー]
Guangzhou Toyota Motor. [Auto manufactures]
CD: 宗形英作　Eisaku Munakata
CD, AD: 日髙英輝　Eiki Hidaka
AD: イシザキ ミチヒロ　Michihiro Ishizaki
D: 杉山紘一　Koichi Sugiyama
P: 数井啓介　Keisuke Kazui
CW: 刘立 波　Liu Libo
PLANNER: 庭山裕之 Hiroyuki Niwayama / 鐘 鳴　Ming Zhong
DIGITAL ARTIST: 村山輝代　Teruyo Murayama
DF, SB: ドッポ　doppo inc.

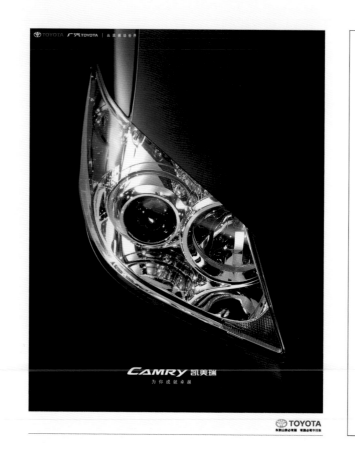

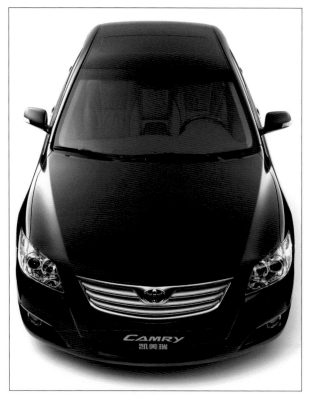

www.guangzhoutoyota.com.cn 广州丰田汽车有限公司 客户服务中心: 800-8308888 (免费热线)

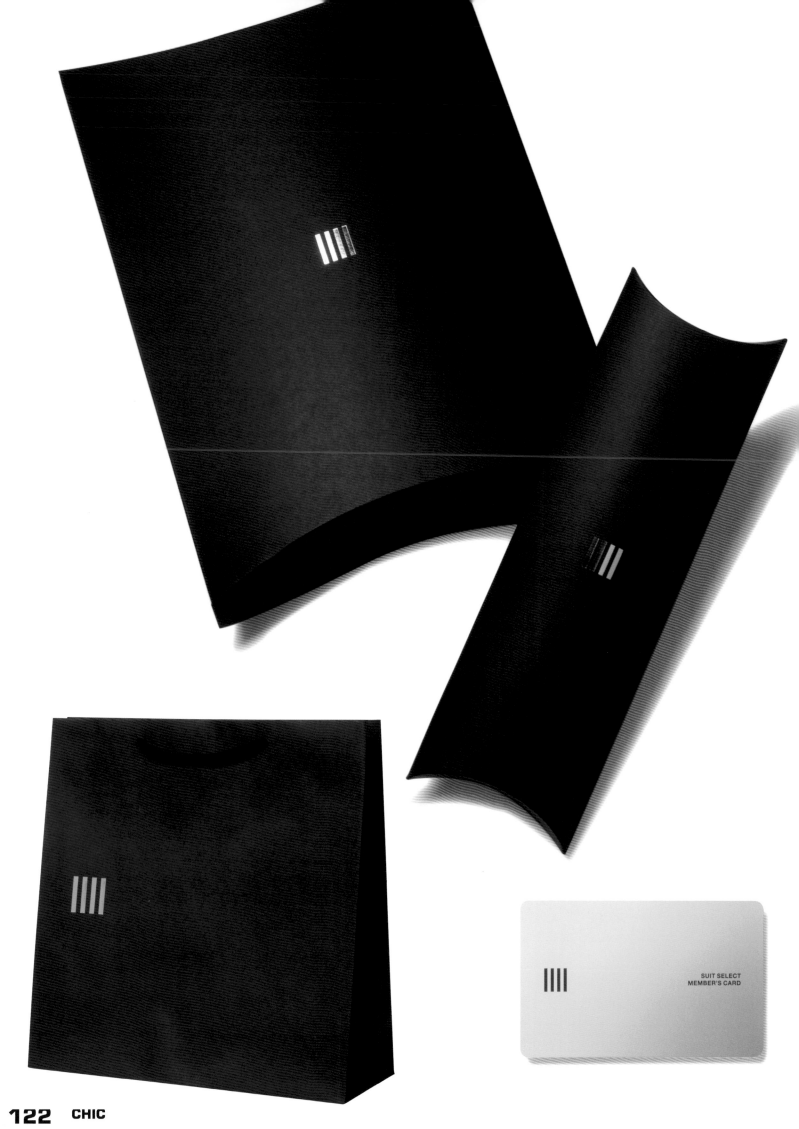

SUIT SELECT
MEMBER'S CARD

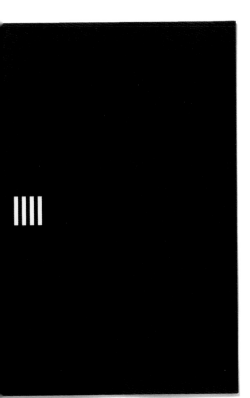

|||| BLACK LINE

その時々のスーツの潮流（トレンド）を取り入れつつ、さらに素材や各部のデザインを進化させることで機能性と美しさの完成度を高めた、いわば「ハイ・コンテンポラリー」を基軸とするライン。今回は、「スリム」「シャープ」「直線的」をキーワードに、シルエットの立体性や新素材の採用など細部まで工夫を重ねることで、タイト感を楽しみながらも抜群の着やすさ・動きやすさを体感できる仕上がりになっています。

The Black Line interprets the latest trends in suits through superior materials and design for a complete combination of function and style. Based on the concept of "high contemporary," the key words for the Black Line are: slim, sharp and straight-edged. The solid, silhouetted outlines, new materials and attention to detail make today's tight look surprisingly easy to wear and move in.

|||| SUIT SELECT_BLACK LINE : SUIT ¥29,400 SHIRTS ¥4,095 TIE ¥3,045 SHOES ¥12,600

パッケージ、ショップバッグ、カタログ / PACKAGE, SHOP BAG, CATALOGUE

コナカ ［アパレル］
Konaka ［Apparel］
CD, AD: 佐藤可士和　Kashiwa Sato
D: 石川 耕　Ko Ishikawa / 江藤 源　Gen Eto /
　　笠原智敦　Tomoatsu Kasahara
SB: サムライ　Samurai Inc.

ショップオープニング案内状 / SHOP OPENING INVITATON

ビームス ［セレクトショップ］
BEAMS Co.,Ltd. ［Speciality shop］
CD: 長友美恵子　Mieko Nagatomo
AD, D: 坂田友紀　Yuki Sakata
SB: ビームスクリエイティブ　BEAMS CREATIVE Inc.

A▲ STYLERS

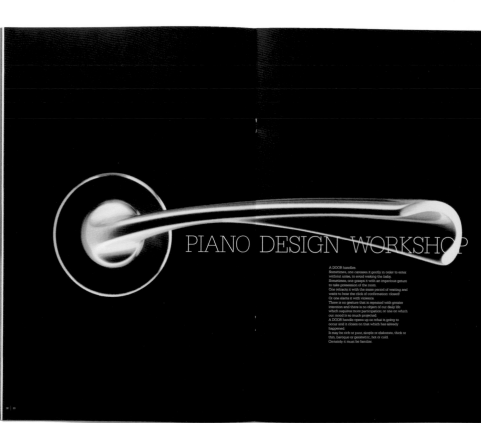

PIANO DESIGN WORKSHOP

A DOOR handles.
Sometimes, one caresses it gently in order to enter without noise, to avoid waking the baby.
Sometimes, one grasps it with an imperious gesture to take possession of the room.
One retracts it with the same period of waiting and waits to hear the click of confirmation: closed!
Or one slams it with violence.
There is no gesture that is repeated with greater intention and there is no object of our daily life which requires more participation; or one on which our mood is so much projected.
A DOOR handle opens up on what is going to occur and it closes on that which has already happened.
It may be rich or poor, simple or elaborate, thick or thin, baroque or geometric, hot or cold.
Certainly it must be familiar.

01

H350R8
¥55,650 (¥53,000)
MATERIAL : brass FINISH : cromsatin

I see it if I decide to look at it. I just caress it or grip it strongly several times a day. It opens all doors. I look at it with the fondness I reserve for all objects having a precise function. The handle which reveals deeply the culture of the environment.

02

H344R8
¥64,050 (¥61,000)
MATERIAL : brass FINISH : cromsatin

That's what I call a basic, elementary object, the zero degree of design. A minimal solution to give personality to a door, to a window.
Its elementary shapes have a natural logic to my architectural approach.

03

H343R8
¥35,700 (¥34,000)
MATERIAL : brass FINISH : cromsatin

I am interested in architecture which offers a total vision. Everything must be considered as anything which you place in a space has an impact. Design for me is about a process of refining and reducing, to reach the point of perfect clarity where form and function coincide.

04

H335R8
¥37,800 (¥36,000)
MATERIAL : brass FINISH : cromo

Extending the language of form that has defined Richard Meier's architecture, the RM Novecento series for Fusital fuses elemental curves, rectangles and squares into hardware designed to both complement and enhance a variety of environments.

05

K328R8
¥44,100 (¥42,000)
MATERIAL : brass FINISH : cromo

06

H333R8Y
¥32,550 (¥31,000)
MATERIAL : brass FINISH : nikmatt

A door handle opens up on what is going to occur and it closes on that which has already happened. It may be rich or poor, simple or elaborate, thick or thin, baroque or geometric, hot or cold. Certainly it must be familiar.

07

H5011R8
¥75,600 (¥72,000)
MATERIAL : stainless FINISH : lucido

08

H338R8
¥22,050 (¥21,000)
MATERIAL : brass FINISH : cromsatin

President of Kono Designs, design firm. Received a degree in architecture at Tama Art University in Tokyo in 1981. Worked on showrooms for Radio Artemide and Poltrona Frau, set designed for Radio Televisione Italiana. Awarded from the Japan Display and Sign Design Associations.

DESIGNERS

01 ジェルレ・アソシエイツ
Cerri&Associati

1971年にグレゴッティアソシアティ・インテルナツィオナルの創設メンバーとなり、その後B&B Italia、Poltrona Frau、Thonet等のデザインを手掛ける。コンパッソ・ドーロ賞を2回受賞。

02 ジャン・ヌーベル
Jean Nouvel

アラブ世界研究所の建物で一躍脚光を浴びる。ガラスなど透過性のある素材と大胆に用い、透視的な効果をもつ幻想的な作品を作り出す際の作品、しばしばVanishing architecture（消失する建築）とも呼ばれている。

03 ジョン・ポーソン
John Pawson

ミニマリストとして世界的に著名なデザイナー。作品Bruce Chatwinの邸宅やCalvin Kleinのショップ（店舗）、Cathay Pacific航空のラウンジ（香港内）などを手掛け、世界的な注目を集めている。

04, 05 リチャード・マイヤー
Richard Meier

欧米を中心に、コードハウスや公共の建物などを手掛ける。コスグーピスろのゲッティセンター、フランクフルトの装飾美術館、バルセロナ現代美術館と、建築界の権威ある賞「プリツカー賞」を1984年に受賞。

06, 07 ピアノデザイン
Piano Design Workshop

ジェノバとパリにセンター、ベルリンにオフィスを置き手掛ける。24時間の建築家活動に入り、美術館の建築家設計ロゼロベ、ゴールドメダル、アメリカ建築家協会の設計会員を、2001年には高名のウェックエーフ賞を受賞。

08 河野 結美
Yoshimi Kono

ニューヨークを拠点に活躍中の建築家。多摩美術大学卒業後、コノデザイン事務所を設立。1984年にDDAデザイン賞、NDAを1984年に1992年に受賞。

09, 10 アントニオ・チッテリオ
Antonio Citterio

ハックマン、フロス、ヴィトラ、B&B、カルテルなどとのコラボレーションを通じ、数多くの家具やデザインアイテムを手掛ける。企業用のデザイン業界に多大な影響を与える数多く。コンパッソ・ドーロ賞など受賞数多数。

11 マッシミリアーノ・フクサス
Massimiliano E Doriana Fuksas

パリ建築大学客員教授。ロカとビド大学客員教授も歴任。クインタンヌ（ヴィーニ）、フェラーリサーチセンター、エンゾフェラーリ・アルマーニ（香港）など代表作が多数。ミラノの新しい見本市会場（フィエラ）の設計が話題に。

12 ドローグデザイン
Droog Design Ronald Lewerissa

1993年ミラノサローネで一連のデザイン活動を発表し、脚光を浴びたオランダのデザインユニット。精鋭のデザイナー、キュレーターが連携して、その時々で選んだメンバーを擁して発表する新制な活動は、つねにデザイン界の注目の的である。

13 リチャード・ボフィル
Richardo Bofill

都市計画的なグローバルな視点を持つ建築家として、世界各国の都市計画に参加。数々の建築は、classicな表現をベースに、それをmodernにアレンジさせる等、それぞれの穏やかなイタリア気と環境への配慮により、世界的な注目を集めている。

14, 15 フォスター&パートナー
Foster & Partner

マンチェスター大学で建築学及び都市計画を学び、「建築は芸術と科学の融合」をベースに、世界中で100を超える多様なプロジェクトを手掛ける。洗練された、いかにも彼の環境への配慮により、世界的な注目を集めている。

16 Fusital

 フジタルワークショップ
Fusital Workshop

30年にわたり常に同時代の最重要デザイナーを起用し、金属製造を企画するトップデザインブランド「フジタル」。自社のデザイン部門により、シンプルであからにイタリア風なこだわった商品を送り出し続けている。

09

H326R8
¥17,850 (¥17,000)
MATERIAL : brass FINISH : cromsatin

My work on handles involves the redesign of classic models studying the small details and new proportions which them become the characteristic elements.

10

H5015R8
¥51,450 (¥49,000)
MATERIAL : stainless FINISH : lucido

11

H5020R8
¥35,700 (¥34,000)
MATERIAL : stainless FINISH : satinato

Emotions, images, sensations...these are alive in our projects from the largest to the smallest.
The object is changeable, far from the gravity of architecture. Models, casts, trials are the setting in which the simplicity, the essentiality, the functionality of our project live together.

12

H5019R8
¥69,300 (¥66,000)
MATERIAL : stainless FINISH : satinato

Droog Design was firstly in the spotlight by presenting a series of design activities at Milano Salone in 1993. Their novel activities, teaming up with superior world designers and curators at every moment, are always in the center of attention in the design industry.

13

H5008R8
¥35,700 (¥34,000)
MATERIAL : stainless FINISH : satinato

The design lies particularly in the joint between the pin element and the handle itself, a joint which is inspired by the structural joining of metallic profiles, with the object of harmonizing all of the component elements. It is a simple and rigorous

14

H5007LR8
¥81,900 (¥78,000)
MATERIAL : stainless + pear wood
FINISH : satin / pear wood

I was intrigued by the handle to the door, which was cast in metal in the form of a stylized bird. It was not only good to look at. More important was the way it sat in the hand. The handle of a door could be linked to architecture in miniature.

15

K5304R8
¥33,600 (¥32,000)
MATERIAL : stainless FINISH : satinato

16

K5302R8
¥23,100 (¥22,000)
MATERIAL : stainless FINISH : satinato

For 30 years, always appointing the most important designers at the time. Leading top brand 'Fusital' in metal fittings industry. In house design department suggests products which are simple and designed details with care.

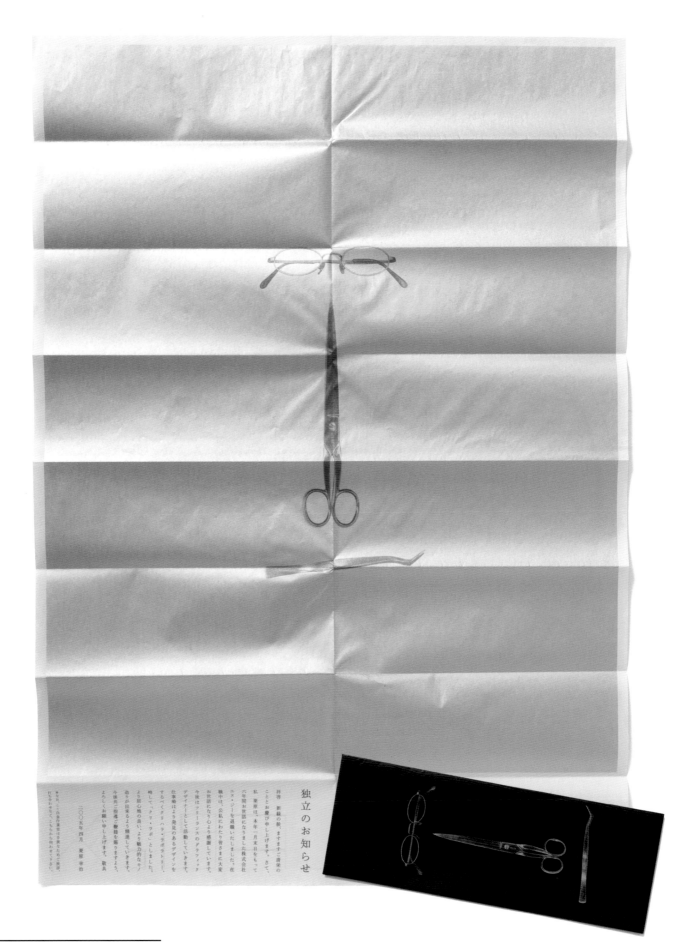

独立のお知らせ

拝啓　新緑の候、ますますご清栄のこととお慶び申し上げます。さて、私事ですが、本年一月末日をもちまして六年間お世話になりました株式会社エヌ・シーを退職いたしました。在職中は、公私にわたり皆さまに大変お世話になり心より感謝いたしております。今後はフリーランスのグラフィックデザイナーとして活動していきます。仕事場はより発見のあるデザインをするべく「クリ・ラボ」としました。名称しクリ・ハラ・ラボラトリーより別に趣の良い、より魅力的なモノ造りが出来るよう精進していきますよう、今後ともご指導ご鞭撻を賜りますよう、よろしくお願い申し上げます。敬具

二〇〇五年四月　栗原幸治

なお、この二か月程度はご連絡打ちが叶わなくてこちらから伺いさせていただきます。

商品案内カタログ /
PRODUCT PROMOTION CATALOGUE

阿部興業 ［木製建具の専門メーカー］
Abe Kogyo Co.,Ltd. [Wood fixture specialty maker]
CD, AD: 久住欣也 [Hd Lab Inc.]　Yoshinari Hisazumi [Hd Lab Inc.]
D: 坂口智彦 [Hd Lab Inc.]　Tomohiko Sakaguchi [Hd Lab Inc.]
P: 初沢克利 （表紙）　Katsutoshi Hatuzawa
CW: 宮崎 真 [モノタイプ]　Makoto Miyazaki [monotype]
DF, SB: Hd Lab Inc.　Hd Lab Inc.

事務所設立の案内状 /
OFFICE ORGANIZE INVITATION

クリ・ラボ ［デザイン事務所］
KURI-LAB. [Design office]
AD, D: 栗原幸治　Koji Kurihara
DF, SB: クリ・ラボ　KURI-LAB.

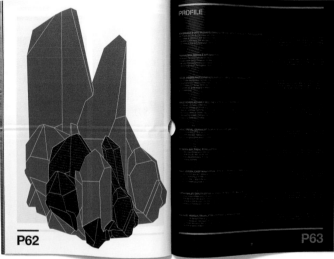

BLACK IS BACK AND
SO IS TOMORROW!

AS WITH THE COLOUR BLACK YOU
MIGHT EXPECT TO BE GREETED
A CONSERVATIVE, YET ELEGANT AND
HIGHLY DISCERNABLE TOMORROW
NEVERTHELESS TOMORROW HAS
EVOLVED AND TAKEN ON NOT ONLY A
NEW AND MORE POWERFUL COVER
BUT ALSO A WHOLE NEW WAY OF
PRESENTING ITS CONTENT.

カルチャーマガジン / FASHION TREND PUBLICATION

Bestseller/Stylecounsel ［アパレル］	
Bestseller/Stylecounsel [Fashion Industry]	
CD: Per Madsen	
STRATEGIC CD: Jesper von Wieding	
ACCOUNT DIRECTOR: Anne _ Mette Højland	
SB: Scandinavian DesignLab	

アートブック / ART BOOK

cry out for joy, you lower parts of the earth ［書籍］
cry out for joy, you lower parts of the earth ［Book］
D: YB- in cooperation with Karin van Dam
SB: Karin Van Dam

イベント案内状 / IVENT INVITATON

LEON［雑誌］
LEON［Magazine］
AD: 久住欣也　Yoshinari Hisazumi
D: 小野美名子［Hisazumi design］(DM)　Minako Ono [Hisazumi design Inc.](DM) /
　原田 諭[Hisazumi design](紙幣 コイン)　Satoru Harada [Hisazumi design Inc.](Paper money Coin)
PLANNER: 熊谷 透[LEON]　Toru Kumagai [LEON]
EVENT CONDUCT: エグゼク インターナショナル　EXEC.INTERNATIONAL INC.
DF, SB: Hisazumi design　Hisazumi design Inc.

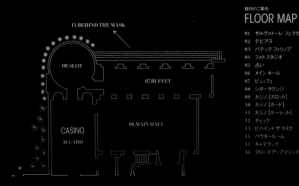

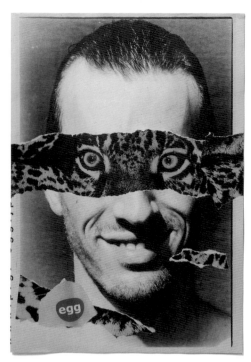

冊子／BOOKLET

横浜ゴム (PRGR) [ゴルフメーカー]
The Yokohama Rubber Company, Limited [Golf Manufacturer]
CD, CW: 三井浩　Hiroshi Mitsui
AD: 永井裕明　Hiroaki Nagai
D: 藤井圭　Kei Fujii
P: 市川勝弘　Katsuhiro Ichikawa
PR: 金尾泰雄　Yasuo Kanao
DF, SB: エヌ・ジー　N.G.INC.,

非 常 識 な 計 算 。

ドライバーを使う回数は、一般的に14回。アイアンは、パーオンを原則にパー5で2打、3打とアイアンを使うと仮定すると、22回打つことになる。仮にドライバーの飛距離が10ヤード伸びると、10×14で合計140ヤードの効果があるが、アイアンで同じ距離を伸ばすと、全体で220ヤードの余裕が生まれる。飛距離で悩む人は、20ヤード伸ばせればさらに倍、440ヤード助かる計算だ。100%の力でキリギリの飛距離を狙おうとすると、アイアンのミスは多発する。アイアンは、決まった距離を打つためのクラブである。手にしたアイアンが飛ぶとわかっていれば、メチャ振りはなくなる（はずだ）。ドライバーは、どこまでも飛ばしていいクラブだからそうはいかない。従って、いま使っているアイアンを飛距離の出るアイアンに持ち替えることは、飛びのドライバーを使用するより、数字的にも、精神的にも、アドバンテージは、大きいことになる。飛距離というとドライバーと常識的に考えがちだが、非常識な発想がゴルフを大きく変えることもある。

170ヤード、何番で打ちますか。

www.prgr-egg.jp

PRGR

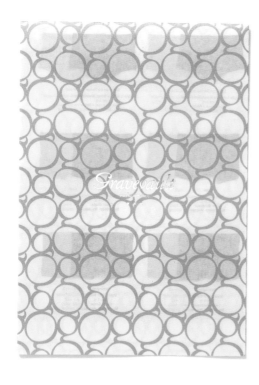

パッケージ、ポスターカタログ /
PACKAGE, POSTER CATALOGUE

ターキー［アパレル］
TuRkey.Co.,Ltd.［Apparel］
AD: 野口孝仁　Takahito Noguchi
D: 駒沢智子　Tomoko Komazawa
DF, SB: ダイナマイト・ブラザーズ・シンジケート
　　　Dynamite Brothers Syndicate

133

ニューアルバムリリースパーティー招待状 /
NEW ALBUM RELEASE PARTY INVITATION

ザディグ　エ　ヴォルテール［アパレル］
Zadig & Voltare ［Apparel］
CD, AD, D: NESCO　NESCO
DF: NIGREC DESIGN　NIGREC DESIGN
SB: モーテル　MOTEL

新店舗オープニングレセプションキッド /
NEW SHOP OPENING RECEPTION KIT

ソスウ インターナシオナル［アパレル］
SOSU international Co.,Ltd.［Apparel］
PR: ソスウ インターナショナル　SOSU international Co.,Ltd.

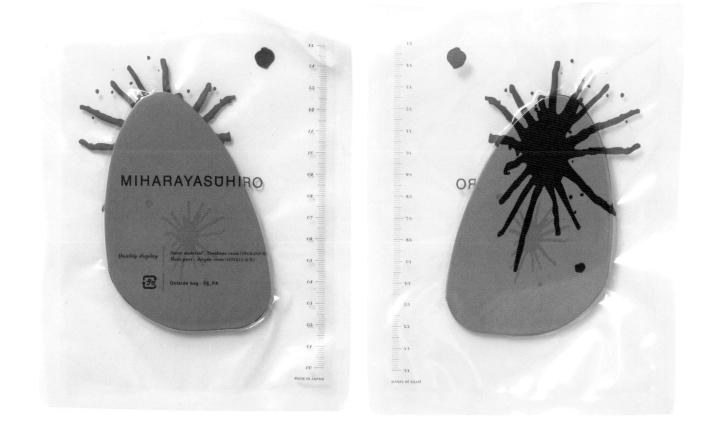

alfredo∞BANNISTER

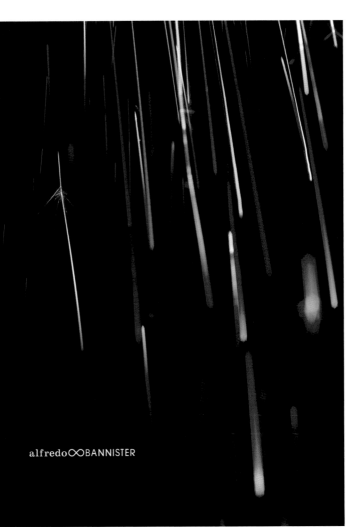

alfredo∞BANNISTER

ブランドポスター ／ BRANDING POSTER

アバハウスインターーナショナル［アパレル］
ABAHOUSE INTERNATIONAL CO. [Apparel]
AD, D: 野尻大作　Daisaku Nojiri
P: 瀧本幹也　Mikiya Takimoto
DF, SB: ground　ground

CD

WARNER MUSIC［音楽制作事業］
WARNER MUSIC [RECORD COMPANY]
CD, AD, D: Paul West
DESGIN ASSITED: KATE PAYNE
DF, SB: Form

パッケージ / PACKAGE

アヴェダ［化粧品製造・販売］
Aveda Corporation [Cosmetics manufacture&sales]
SB: アヴェダ　Aveda Corporation

パッケージ / PACKAGE

H.Krüll&C.spa ［化粧品の製造・販売］
H.Krüll&C.spa ［Cosmetics Manufacture&Sales］
CD, AD, D: Federico Frasson
P: Orlando Bonacdo
SB: FK DEISGN SRL

the 143rd ddd gallery exhibition

Katsunori aoki

XX

2005.09.13(tue) - 10.13(thu)

10:00 a.m. - 6:00 p.m. closed=saturdays / sundays / holidays

ddd gallery dojima axis bldg. 1F 2.2.28 dojimahama kita-ku osaka 530-0208 japan tel 06-6347-8780

gallery talk 09.13(tue) 4:00 p.m. - 5:30 p.m.

ichiro tanida × katsunori aoki

DNP DUO DOJIMA

www.butterfly-stroke.com

パッケージ / PACKAGE

資生堂 ［化粧品の製造・販売］
Shiseido CO.,LTD. [Cosmetics Manufacture&Sales]
CD, AD: 大智 惠　Megumi Ochi
D: 駒井麻郎　Mao Komai
SB: 資生堂　Shiseido CO.,LTD.

展覧会告知ポスター ／
EXHIBITION ANNOUCEMENT POSTER

LDH ［総合エンターテイメント事業］
LDH inc. [General Entertainment Business]
CD, AD, D: 青木克憲　Katsunori Aoki
DF, SB: バタフライ・ストローク　butterfly stroke inc.

展覧会告知ポスター ／
ART EXHIBITION ANNOUCEMENT POSTER

トランスアート ［ギャラリーの運営・出版物の企画制作］
Trans Art Inc. [Gallery]
CD, AD, D: 青木克憲　Katsunori Aoki
DF, SB: バタフライ・ストローク　butterfly stroke inc.

パッケージ / PACKAGE

ペルノリカールジャパン ［飲料品製造・販売］
Pernod Ricard Japan K.K. [Beverage Production and Sales]
AD: 鷲見陽　Akira Sumi
DF, SB: アンテナグラフィックベース
　　　　ANTENNA GRAPHIC BASE CO.,LTD.

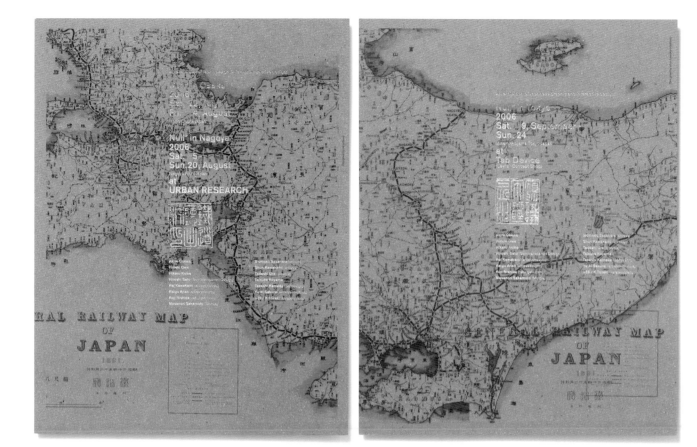

コレクション案内状 / SHOW INVITATION

ヌル™ [グループ]
null™ [Group]
CD, AD, D: 川上 俊 Shun Kawakami
DF, SB: アートレス artless Inc.

5周年記念パーティー案内状 /
5TH ANNIVERSARY PARTY ANNOUNCEMENT

ナノ・ユニバース [セレクトショップ]
nano・Euniverse/ [Speciality Shop]
CD, AD, D: NESCO NESCO
DF: NIGREC DESIGN NIGREC DESIGN
SB: モーテル MOTEL

AVANT-GARDE

Cool / Ironic / Unique
クールな / ひねくれた / ユニークな

Alexander Gelman – a "tough" designer talks about "tough-style" design

What serves as the springboard for your concepts when you design advertising?
I start from analyzing the brief and if necessary modifying it according to my understanding of the situation. Sometimes it's necessary to acquire additional information and/or learn about the client/industry, etc.

What is essential to remember in designing advertising?
To stay on track, keeping focus on the message and the context of this communication.

What points do you stress in order to create design that's strong and communicates?
Energy and impact. The design solution cannot be forced one way or another. Even the most intricate communication must appear as effortless. More like a happy accident than a result of painful process of trial and error.

What is do think critical to designing advertising for a male audience?
Respect of the audience's intelligence.

What effects are you looking to create when you use black?
Black communicates confidence and — when used correctly — is the most luxuries color.

ALEXANDER GELMAN
In 2001 The Museum of Modern Art listed Alexander Gelman among the "world's most influential modern and contemporary artists in all media." Alexander Gelman (simply known as Gelman or Glmn) is based in New York, London and Tokyo. Gelman's print, video and media installations, extensively shown around the world, are represented in permanent museum collections, including the Smithsonian, the New York's MoMA, and Bibliothèque National de France in Paris. Gelman also serves as guest professor at Yale University and MIT Media Lab. He had authored a number of books, articles, and was a subject of several monographs. Among them 'Subtraction', 'Infiltrate' and 'Gelman Thinks.'

His Works / P147

『男』なデザイナーの語る『男』なデザイン／アレクサンダー・ゲルマン
広告（デザイン）を設計する際の発想の出発点は何か
まず依頼内容を分析し、シチュエーションに応じて必要だと感じれば、内容を修正します。クライアントやその業界について、より多くの情報を集めたり、研究したりしなければならない場合もあります。

広告（デザイン）を設計する際に外せない点は
その広告が伝えるべきメッセージや内容に集中し、ぶれないこと。

強くて伝わるデザインを生み出すためのこだわりは何か
エネルギーとインパクト。デザインソリューションは、何かを強いてはなりません。非常に複雑なデザインであっても、簡単に作ったように見えなければなりません。つまり、試行錯誤を繰り返して苦労して作ったものではなく、偶然良いものができてしまったかのように見せるのです。

男性を意識した広告を設計する際に大切にしてる点は
見る人の知性を尊重する。（親切に説明しすぎない）

黒色を使用する際、どんな効果を狙っているのか
黒は信頼／確実性を伝える色であり、正しく使えば、最も高級感の出せる色。

アレクサンダー・ゲルマン
2001年、MOMAが選ぶ『あらゆるメディアにおいて世界で最も影響力のある現代のアーティスト』の一人に選出される。ゲルマンもしくはGLMNとして知られ、NY、ロンドン、東京を拠点に活躍。その作品は世界各国で広く紹介され、スミソニアン協会、NYのMOMA、パリのフランス国立図書館などに永久所蔵されている。イェール大学、MITメディアラボの客員教授も務める。『SUBTRACTION』、『INFILTRATE』、『GELMAN THINKS』など著書多数。

作品掲載ページ／P147

モダン・デザインの世界遺産、バウハウス。

バウハウス・デッサウで一体

ヴァルター・グロビウス

ス・デッサウ＠東京藝術大学大学美術館

こんなバウハウス展、見たことない。

ロイヤー

ラスロ・モホイ＝ナジ

きていたのか?!　こんなバウハウス展、見たことない。　バウハウス・デッサウ＠東京藝術大学

ワシリー・カンディンスキー　パウル・クレー　マルセル・ブロイヤー

バウハウス・デッサウ展
BAUHAUS
experience, dessau
2008.4.26SAT-7.21MON
東京藝術大学大学美術館

主催：東京藝術大学、産経新聞社　共催：バウハウス・デッサウ財団 bauhaus 後援：ドイツ連邦共和国大使館

こんなバウハウス展見たことない！1919年にドイツ、ヴァイマールに誕生した、造形芸術学校・バウハウス。1933年に閉校し、75年経った今も、世界中のデザインや建築に大きな影響を与え続けています。バウハウスはヴァイマール、デッサウ、ベルリンと場所を変え活動していましたが、デッサウの地において創設者ヴァルター・グロピウスの理想が実現したといえましょう。本展は、バウハウスを歴史の中に捉えなおし、デッサウに焦点を当てながら、カンディンスキーやクレーなどマイスターたちによる教育の成果、工房によるプロダクトを紹介します。とりわけ、舞台工房は映像も公開。バウハウスの最終目標であった「建築」に関する資料やマケットも合わせて全体で200点以上の作品を展示します。そのほとんどがバウハウス・デッサウ財団所有の作品であり、日本初公開の作品も少なくありません。また、展覧会のみどころとして、世界遺産にも登録されているデッサウ校舎内の初代校長・ヴァルター・グロピウスの校長室を再現し、実際に体感していただきます。今回の展覧会が改めて、バウハウスの世界に与えた影響やその意味を実感していただける絶好の機会になることは間違いありません。

■ 期間限定発売！ペアチケット（¥2,000）／1月12日（土）〜2月11日（月）ローソンチケット他にて発売。
お問い合わせ　産経新聞社事業部　03-3275-8904（平日のみ）　http://www.bauhaus-dessau.jp

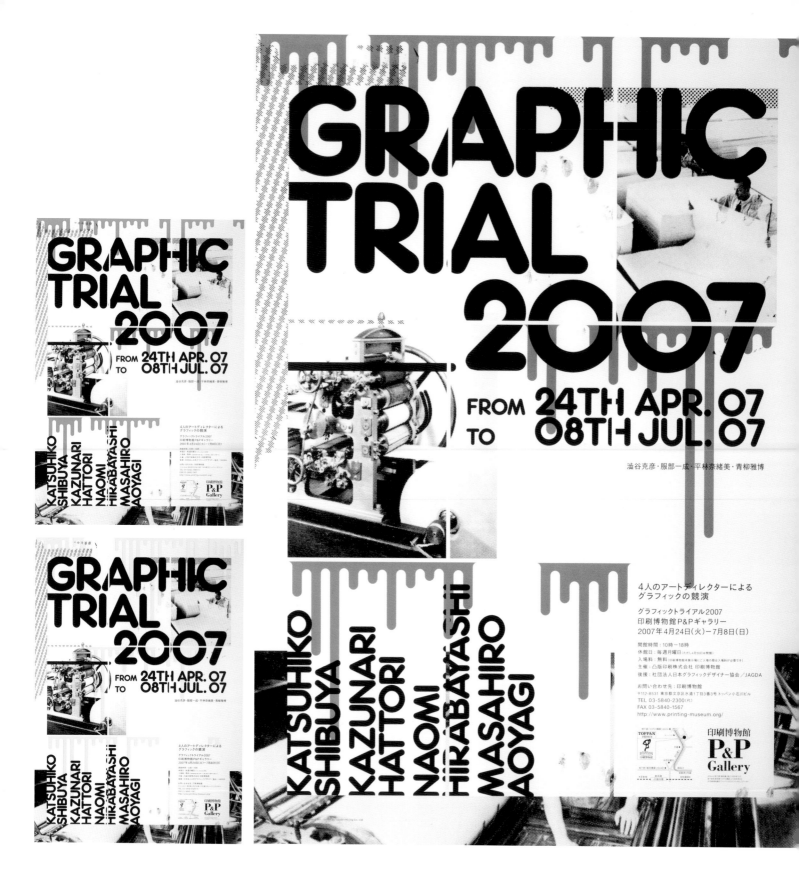

展覧会告知ポスター／
ART EXHIBITION ANNOUNCEMENT POSTER

凸版印刷 ［印刷］
TOPPAN PRINTING CO.,LTD. ［Printing Company］
AD, D: 平林奈緒美　Naomi Hirabayashi
DF, SB: プラグイングラフィック　PLUG-IN GRAPHIC

イベント告知ポスター、案内状／
IVENT ANNOUNCEMENT POSTER, INVITATION

Gelman Lounge / Minimal Tokyo ［イベント］
Gelman Lounge / Minimal Tokyo ［Event］
CD, AD, D, SB: Alexander Gelman

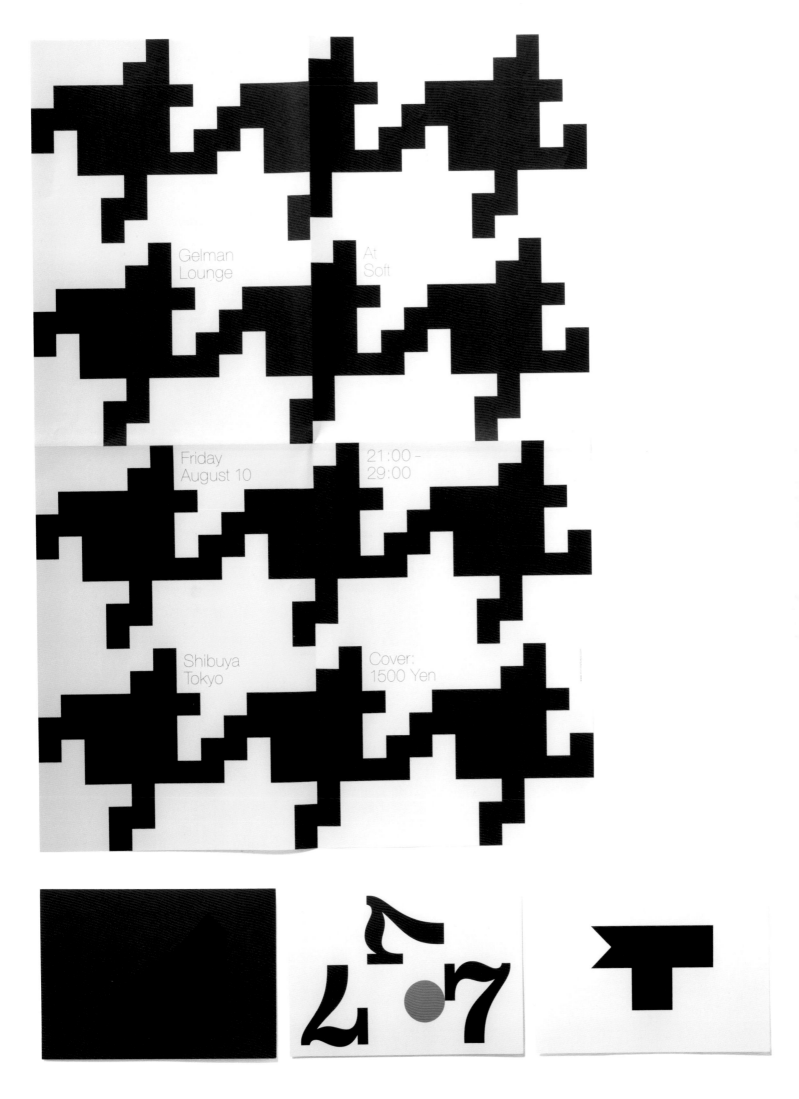

Gelman
Lounge

At
Soft

Friday
August 10

21:00 –
29:00

Shibuya
Tokyo

Cover:
1500 Yen

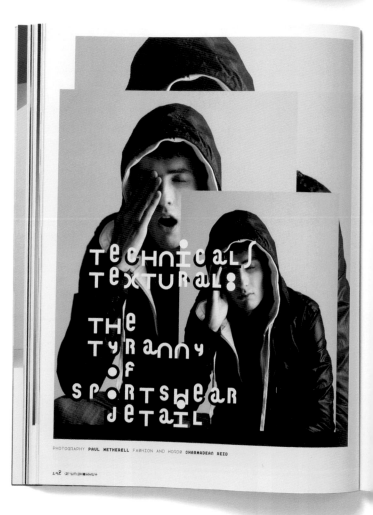

男性誌 / MEN'S MAGAZINE

ARENA HOMME + [男性誌]
ARENA HOMME + [MEN'S MAGAZINE]
CD: Michael Amzalag / Mathias Augus Tyniak
SB: M/M[PARIS]

THE INCREASING insinuation of the blogosphere into all things fashionable is crucial evidence of the solipsistic limits of human sentience, but I'll cut fragrance blogs endless slack. I'm infatuated by the thought of a sweet-smelling gnome sniffing 24/7 at the latest offerings from the world's perfume houses. And God only knows there are enough, veritable hundreds every year. As overwhelmingly commercial as the fragrance business is, the fact that it is hotwired into the human psyche lends it a primal fascination that the fashion industry can't match. I mean, who cares about the width of a lapel when your senses are being sideswiped by an ingredient that toys playfully with your libido?

But I'll admit to a fundamental dissatisfaction with the current state of the men's fragrance industry. So much powder, such a small fuse, and oh! the tiny bang... The powder is, of course, the whacking great reservoir of manstuff that looms behind any manipulation of masculine odour. Here goes. A human being's natural smell is the by-product of his or her apocrine gland system. It produces minute milky secretions which collect in hair follicles. The hair acts like the wick of a candle, wafting the scent around face, head, armpits, groin. And everyone's scent is as distinctive as a fingerprint (honey and violets are two of the more appealing). If there is a male 'essential oil', it's the principal pheromone androstenone, a chemical cousin of testosterone. Found in sweat, tears, urine and hair (particularly genital hair), it can provoke uncontrollable aggression, so fortunately it's imperceptible to a third of the population. It mimics the smell of truffles, which is why lady pigs make such good trufflers. Its perfume equivalent would be a musk.

CLOCKWISE FROM TOP: BLACK CRAMYSKIN BOOT BY TOD'S; BLACK LEATHER TRAINER WITH VELCRO STRAPS BY LOUIS VUITTON; BLACK LEATHER BOOT WITH WOOL TRIM BY GUCCI; BLACK LEATHER LACE-UP BOOT BY CESARE PACIOTTI; SUEDE TRAINER BOOT WITH BLUE STITCH AND LACES BY JOOP; BROWN LEATHER BOOT BY TOM FORD; BLACK SUEDE AND PATENT TRAINER BOOT BY EMPORIO ARMANI.

Information and Catalog: Europe: +33 (0)1 5...

…AYS WHEN synthetic textiles were the poor cousin of …fabrics are long gone. These days, designers choose …according to how well they do the job – particularly in …ar, where design has always been about function rather …coration. Meanwhile, science is increasing the range of …l fabrics available to designers all the time – meaning that …iny, waterproof and makes a rustling sound when you …en it's in favour.

…eachy news to anyone with a …ull of technical sportswear …specialised of specialist clothing …where every design decision is …e-led. Since the late Seventies …hnical casual clothing has been …male obsession – not least …illeurs men to talk about fashion …masculine terms, letting them play …s with spec sheets as opposed to …emlines and celebrities. And it …d a level of obsession at least as …h as that enjoyed by Savile Row, …he tog rating of down and the …el of de-veined feathers is …ent from debates over tent …stitches per inch. Technical …e an appeal to the obsessive …t of men,' says Andrew Bunney, …ager of high-end casualwear …stributor Comme S. 'It takes it …being just "fashion" and becomes …more permanent".

…ccupations have enjoyed a …y devoted following in the north …cause clothes have to work …der in the harsher climate. …ware seeking stylish protection …m Osti's Stone Island and CP …and hankering after other classic …m his short-lived Lefthand …erefore the south woke up to its …all-terrain appeal. And now a …ation of designers – most notably …upe (from Blackburn, or Burnley, …, really) – is reevaluating this …sual tradition. Tokyo has also long …chnical fashion, and many of its …erated streetwear labels have …ed with outdoor textile specialists. …e Japanese label famed for its …hree, shoes, is now venturing into …, with Gore-Tex-treated pea coats …Tweed jackets.

…LISH WATERPROOF COAT BY MASSIMO OSTI LEFTHAND; WHITE COTTON T-SHIRT BY TOPMAN; MOSS GREEN WOOL JUMPER BY CP COMPANY; NAVY GILET BY MONCLER; …CK SUPERFINE NYLON JACKET BY DIESEL; WHITE LEATHER ZIP-UP HOODED TOP BY K-SWISS; STITCHED GREEN AND BROWN POLO SHIRT BY LACOSTE; BLACK WOOL ZIP-UP …DED HOODIE; BLUE DENIM JEANS BY PEPE.

PHOTOGRAPHY MARCUS GAAD EDIT TAMARA ROTHCTEZN CLOCKWISE FROM TOP: LUC CHRONO-DINE WATCH WITH BLACK FACE, TURNING BEZEL AND BLACK STRAP WITH WHITE STITCH BY CHOPARD; LIMITED-EDITION PLATINUM BLUE DIAL WATCH WITH BLACK MOVEN STRAP BY BEDAT + CO.; L'IVE COLOGNE S WATCH WITH TURNING BEZEL, BLACK FACE AND PLATINUM BRACELET BY TAG HEUER; AQUANAUT REF 5164A WATCH WITH BLACK FACE AND BLACK RUBBER STRAP BY PATEK PHILIPPE; TYPE DEMENGED PLATINUM STRAP WATCH WITH BLACK FACE BY BELL + ROSS; SCUBA CHRONO STEEL WATCH WITH THREE DIAL BLACK FACE, STEEL CASE AND BRACELET BY BULGARI.

149

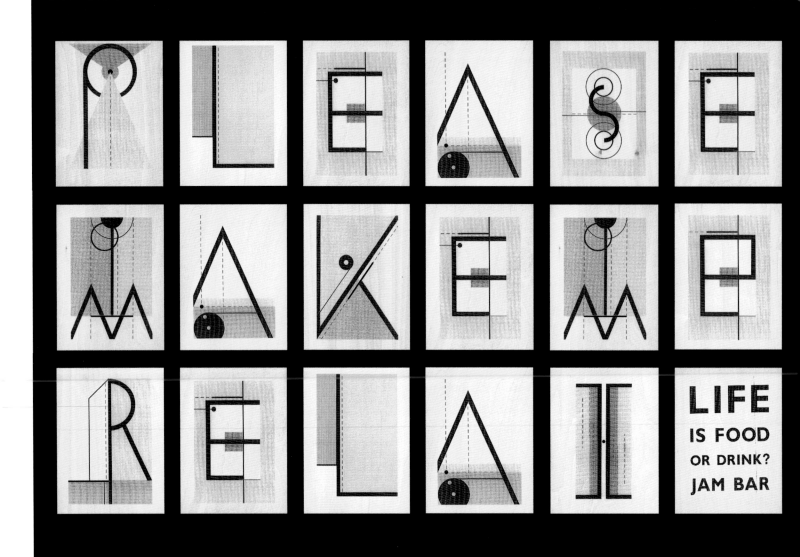

展覧会告知ポスター /
ART EXHIBITION ANNOUNCEMENT, POSTER

森美術館 [美術館]
Mori Art [Museum]
CD, AD: 水野学　Manabu Mizuno
D: 相澤千晶　Chiaki Aizawa
DF, SB: グッドデザインカンパニー　good design company co., ltd.

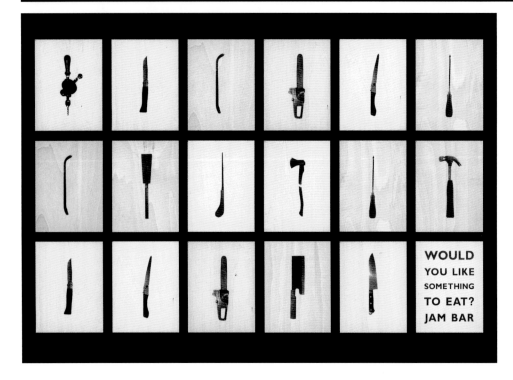

ブランドポスター / BRANDING POSTER

バー・ジャム [飲食店]
Bar JAM [Bar]
AD, D: 小林洋介　Yosuke Kobayashi
SB: イー　E.Co.,Ltd.

151

Kunsthaus Zug mobil [展覧会]
Kunsthaus Zug mobil [Exhibitions]
AD: Ueli Kleeb / Caroline Lotscher
DF, SB: DNS-Transport GmbH

イベント告知ポスター、カタログ、店舗設計 /
EVENT POSTER, CATALOGUE, SHOP DESIGN

DANCE 4/NOTTDANCE ［コンテンポラリーダンスフェスティバル］
DANCE 4/NOTTDANCE ［CONTEMPORARY DANCE FESTIVAL］
CD, AD, D: DAVID BAILEY
DF, SB: KIOSK

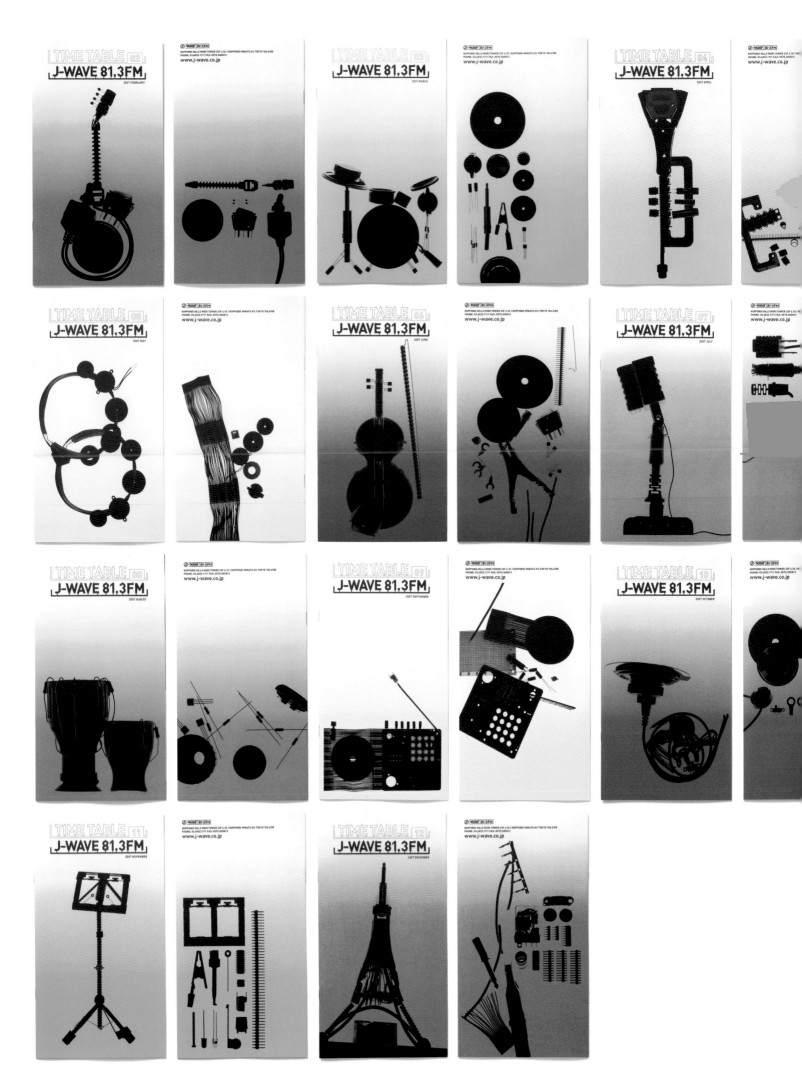

TIME TABLE 01
J-WAVE 81.3FM
2007JANUARY

J-WAVE 81·3FM
ROPPONGI HILLS MORI TOWER 33F 6.10.1 ROPPONGI MINATO.KU TOKYO 106.6188
PHONE: 03.6832.1111 FAX: 0570.000813
www.j-wave.co.jp

タイムテーブル / TIME TABLE

J-WAVE ［放送局］
J-WAVE,INC. ［Broadcasting］
AD: 平林奈緒美　Naomi Hirabayashi
D, P: 米山菜津子　Natsuko Yoneyama
DF, SB: プラグイングラフィック　PLUG-IN GRAPHIC

Motel 2007/2008 Autumn/winter Coll

シーズンコレクション案内状 /
SEASONAL COLLECTION DM

モーテル ［アパレル］
MOTEL ［Apparel］
CD, AD, D: NESCO NESCO
DF: NIGREC DESIGN NIGREC DESIGN
SB: モーテル MOTEL

イベントポスター / IVENT IDENTITY POSTER

BRITISH EMBASSY, TOKYO [展覧会]
BRITISH EMBASSY, TOKYO [Exhibition]
CD, AD, D: PAUL WEST / PAUL BENSON
D: NICK HARD / ANDY HARVEY
P: SPIROS POLITIS
DF, SB: Form

Is it black or white?

Indecisive people make bad designers.

SCHOOL OF DESIGN 01

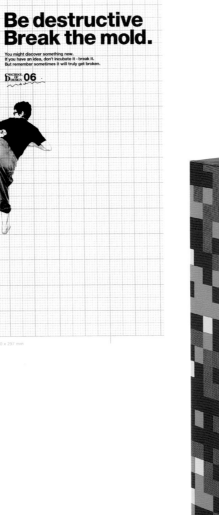

Be destructive Break the mold.

You might discover something new.
If you have an idea, don't incubate it - break it.
But remember sometimes it will truly get broken.

SCHOOL OF DESIGN **06**

A4 210 x 297 mm

展覧会ポスター ／ ART EXHIBITION POSTER

銀座グラフィックギャラリー［ギャラリー］
GINZA GRAPHIC GALLERY [Gallery]
AD, D: 平林奈緒美　Naomi Hirabayashi
DF, SB: プラグイングラフィック　PLUG-IN GRAPHIC

ポスターケース ／ POSTER CASE

日本グラフィックデザイナー協会［デザイン団体］
Japan Graphic Designer Association Inc.［Design Organization］
AD, D: 野尻大作　Daisaku Nojiri
DF, SB: ground　ground

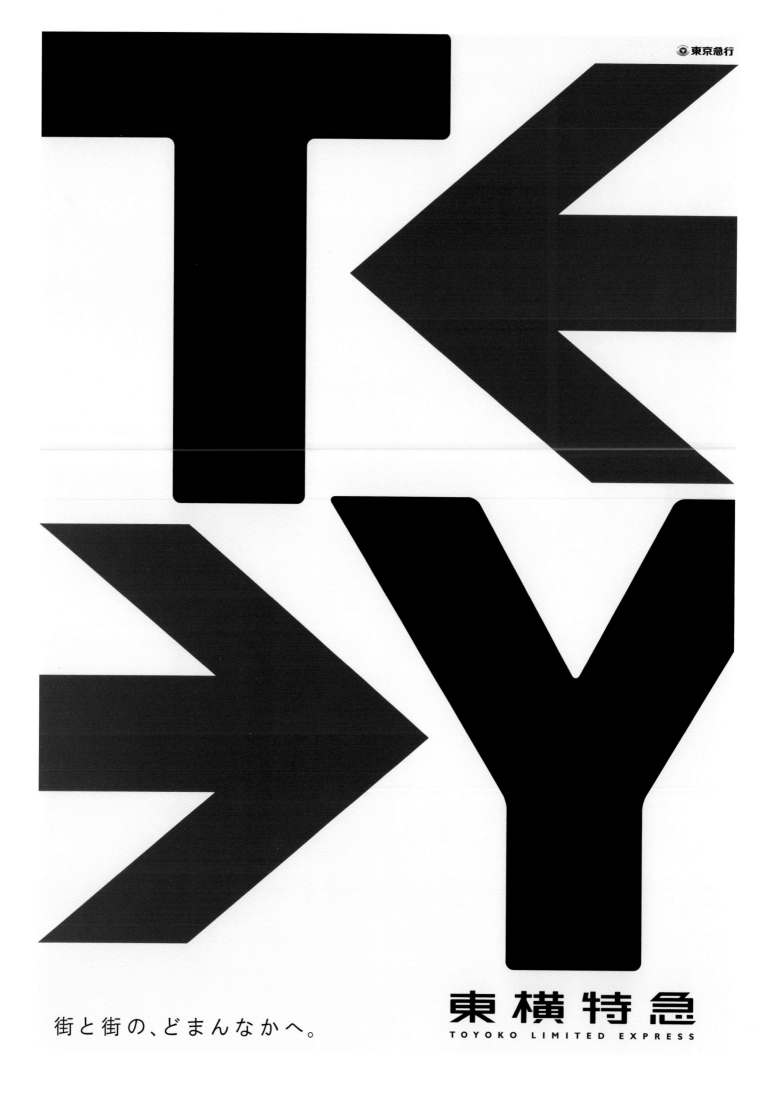

街と街の、どまんなかへ。

東横特急
TOYOKO LIMITED EXPRESS

展覧会ポスター ／ ART EXHIBITION POSTER

ソウル・東京24時／日韓デザイナーの交流展 [展覧会]
Seaul tokyo 24 [EXHIBITION]
AD, D：齋藤 浩　Hiroshi Saito
DF, SB：トンプー・グラフィクス　tong-poo graphics

企業ブランドポスター ／
COMPANY BRANDING POSTER
東京急行電鉄 [電鉄]
TOKYU CORPORATION [Electric railroad company]
CD, AD：日髙英輝　Eiki Hidaka
D：竹林一茂　Kazushige Takebayashi
CW：荻野 綾　Aya Ogino
DF, SB：グリッツデザイン　gritzdesign inc.

公演案内ポスター ／
PERFORMANCE INFORMATION POSTER

トウインクルコーポレーション ［劇団］
TWINKLE Corporation Ltd. [Theater]
CD, AD, TY-PO DIRECTOR: 水野 学　Manabu Mizuno
D: 上村 昌　Masaru Uemura
P: 黒澤康成　Yasunari Kurosawa
TY-PO DIRECTOR: 飯田竜太　Ryuta Iida
DF, SB: グッドデザインカンパニー　good design company co., ltd.

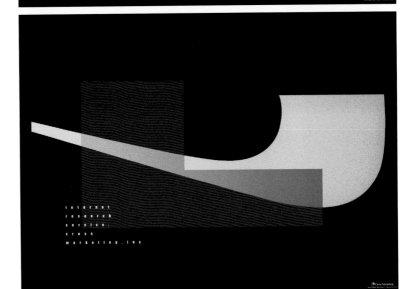

ÉDIFICE

"BUILD AND DESTROY" SERIES JIGSAW PUZZLE

Ref. Number:
00004
Manufacturer:

No of Pieces:
6
Dimensions:
8.7cm × 14cm / 3.42" × 5.51"
Puzzle Type:
Standard Jigsaws
Description:
A highly detailed puzzle with
a image of Mark II "Pineapple"
Grenade.
Suitable for age six and above.

© TAKEO PAPER SHOW 2007
ÉDIFICE × TAKEO
ART WORK: NOB
ART DIRECTION: NAOMI HIRABAYASHI

ノベルティ / NOVELTY

竹尾ペーパーショウ2007 ［紙卸商の展示会］
Takeo Co.,Ltd. [Paper Merchant Exhibition]
AD, D: 平林奈緒美　Naomi Hirabayashi
DF, SB: プラグイングラフィック　PLUG-IN GRAPHIC

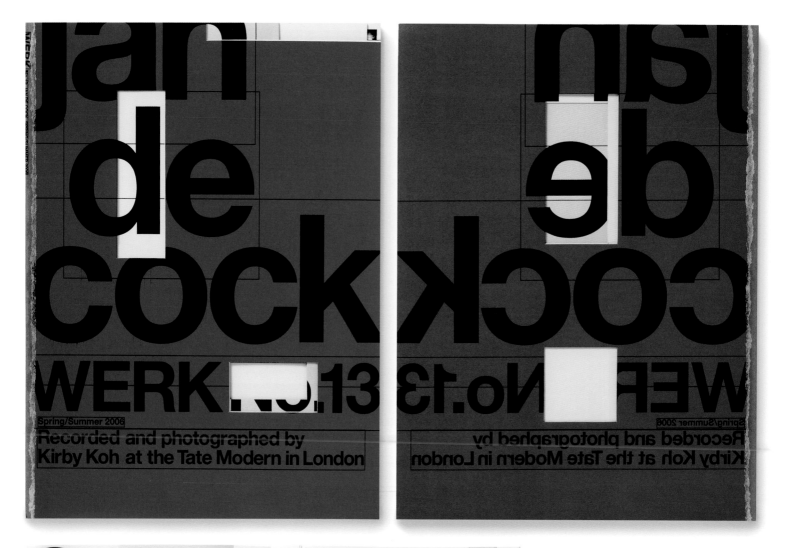

jan
de
cock
WERK No.13
Spring/Summer 2008
Recorded and photographed by
Kirby Koh at the Tate Modern in London

アートマガジン / ART MAGAZINE

WERK MAGAZINE　[アートマガジン]
WERK MAGAZINE　[Art magazine]
CD, D: THESEUS CHAN
AD: MARINA LIM
DF, SB: WORK

イベント告知ポスター /
EVENT ANNOUNCEMENT POSTER

MUZIEKLAB BRABANT　[劇団]
MUZIEKLAB BRABANT　[Theater]
D, SB: Hans Gremmen

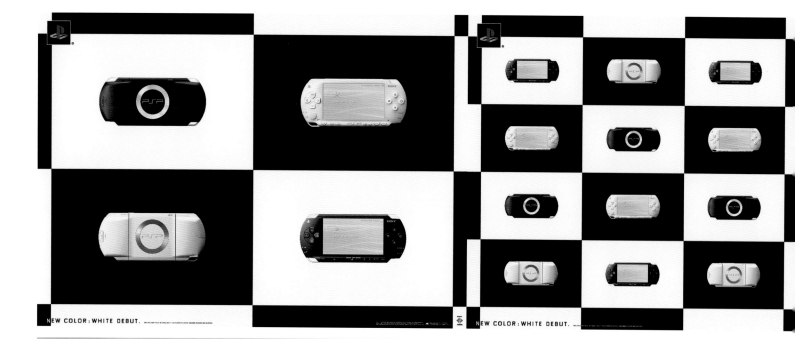

商品案内ポスター、空間演出 /
PRODUCT PROMOTION POSTER, SPACE DIRECTION

ソニー・コンピュータエンタテイメント
[ゲーム機、ソフトウェアの企画・製造・販売]
Sony Computer Entertainment Japan [Research & Development,
production and sales of hardware & software for game machine]
CD: 北見 勝　Masaru Kitami
AD: 佐野研二郎　Kenjiro Sano
D: 小杉幸一　Koichi Kosugi / 本多絵梨　Eri Honda
CW: 斉藤賢司　Kenji Saito / 坪井 卓　Suguru Tsuboi
SB: 博報堂　HAKUHODO Inc. / MR_DESIGN　MR_DESIGN

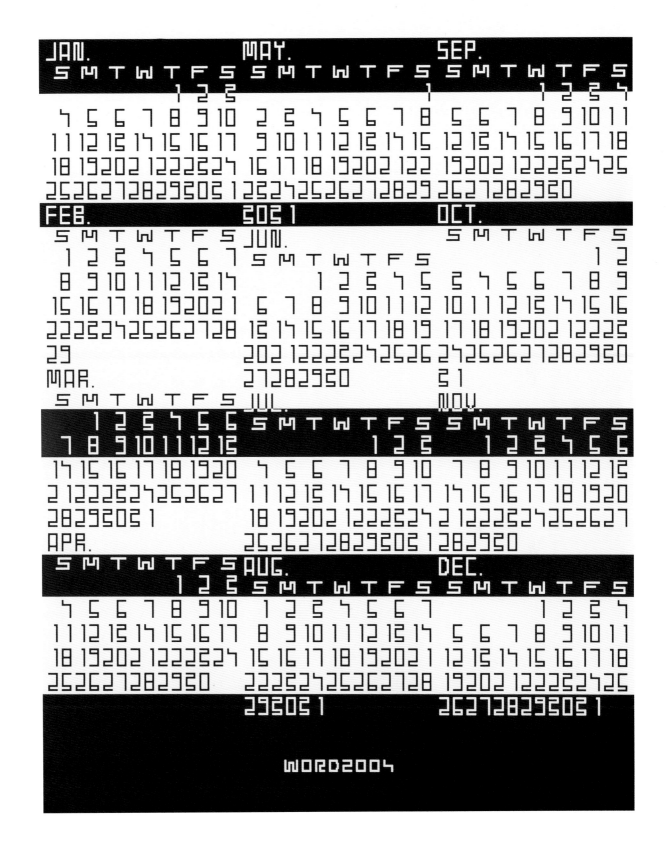

WORD2004

WORD2004

カレンダー / CALENDAR

資生堂 ［化粧品の製造・販売］
Shiseido CO.,LTD. [Cosmetics Manifacture & Sales]
AD, D: 仲條正義　Masayoshi Nakajo
DF, SB: 仲條デザイン事務所　Nakajo Design Office

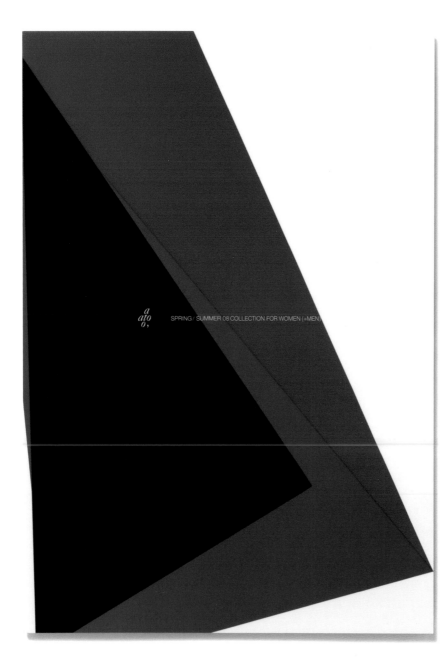

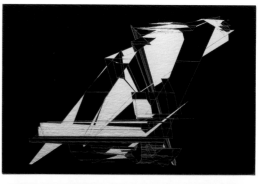

シーズンコレクション案内状、カタログ/
SEASONAL COLLECTION DM, CATALOGUE

アトウ［アパレル］
Ato ［Apparel］
AD, D, SB: 米津智之　Tomoyuki Yonezu
P: 中野敬久　Hirohisa Nakano

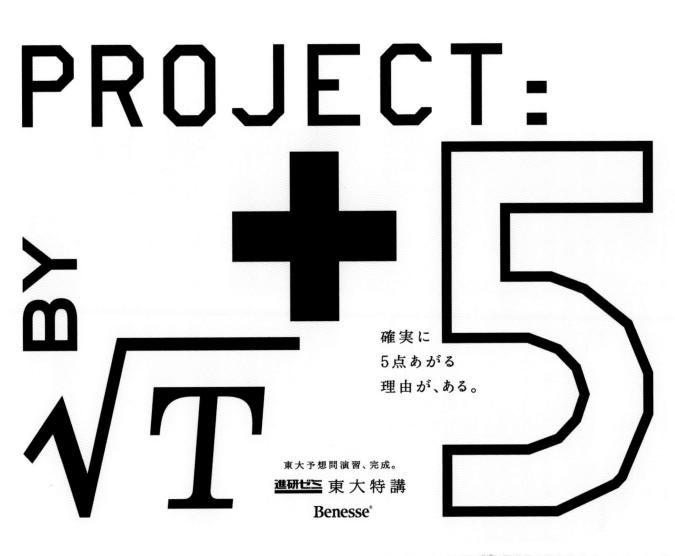

PROJECT:

$$\sqrt{T} + 5$$

BY

確実に
5点あがる
理由が、ある。

東大予想問演習、完成。
進研ゼミ 東大特講
Benesse®

tk.benesse.co.jp

講座案内ポスター、パンフレット /
COURSE INFORMATION POSTER, BROCHURE

ベネッセコーポレーション [教育・出版]
Benesse Corporation [Education&Publishing]
CD, AD: 佐野研二郎　Kenjiro Sano
D: 小杉幸一　Koichi Kosugi
SB: 博報堂　HAKUHODO Inc. / MR_DESIGN　MR_DESIGN

入社案内 / RECRUITMENT BROCHURE

博報堂 [広告代理店]
HAKUHODO Inc. [Advertising agency]
AD, SB: 小杉幸一　Koichi Kosugi
AD: 榮 良太　Ryota Sakae
D: 原野賢太郎　Kentaro Harano / 本多絵梨　Eri Honda /
　中村知美　Tomomi Nakamura
P: 岡 祐介　Yuske Oka
CW: 下東史明　Fumiaki Shimohigashi
DF: シロップ　Syrup

イベント告知ポスター ／
EVENT ANNOUNCEMENT POSTER

Theater Aeternam ［演劇団体］
Theater Aeternam ［Theater Group］
CD, AD, D: Erich Brechbühl
SB: Erich Brechbuhl [Mixer]

何度でも観たくなる、観るたびに病みつきになる至福のリラックス・ワールド。

コーヒー&シガレッツ

ジム・ジャームッシュ監督作品

フライヤー、パンフレット / FLIER, BROCHURE

アスミック・アース・エンターテインメント ［映像配給］
Asmik Ace Entertainment inc. ［Distributing agency］
AD: 駿東 宏　Sunto Hiroshi
D: 土屋かおり　Kaori Tsuchiya
DF, SB: エスジー　SG

COFFEE
AND
CIGARETTES
A FILM BY JIM JARMUSCH

JIM JARMUSCH

ジム・ジャームッシュ［脚本・監督］

ROBERTO BENIGNI STEVEN WRIGHT	JOIE LEE CINQUÉ LEE STEVE BUSCEMI	IGGY POP TOM WAITS	JOE RIGANO VINNY VELLA VINNY VELLA JR.
RENÉE FRENCH E.J. RODRIGUEZ	ALEX DESCAS ISAACH DE BANKOLÉ	CATE BLANCHETT	MEG WHITE JACK WHITE
ALFRED MOLINA STEVE COOGAN	GZA RZA BILL MURRAY	BILL RICE TAYLOR MEAD	COFFEE AND CIGARETTES

REBORN
DEBUT
NEW STAGES
JAN. 05TH, 2006
TAKE OFF
EDOKAWA HEI STUDIO

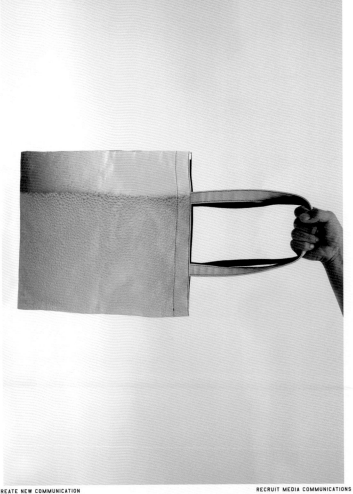

CREATE NEW COMMUNICATION

RECRUIT MEDIA COMMUNICATIONS   CREATE NEW COMMUNICATION

RECRUIT MEDIA COMMUNICATIONS

CREATE NEW COMMUNICATION

RECRUIT MEDIA COMMUNICATIONS   CREATE NEW COMMUNICATION

RECRUIT MEDIA COMMUNICATIONS

施設紹介リーフレット /
FACILITY PRESENTATION LEAFLET

角川大映撮影所 [撮影スタジオ]
KADOKAWA DAIEI STUDIO [Filming Studio]
AD: 永井裕明　Hiroaki Nagai
D: 藤井 圭　Kei Fujii
DF, SB: エヌ・ジー　N.G.INC.

企業ブランドポスター /
COMPANY BRANDING POSTER

リクルート [情報メディアビジネス]
RECRUIT CO., LTD. [Information Media Business]
CD, CW: 日野貴弘　Takahiro Hino
AD: 佐野研二郎　Kenjiro Sano
D: 原野賢太郎　Kentaro Harano
P: 小杉幸一　Koichi Kosugi
SB: 博報堂　HAKUHODO Inc. / MR_DESIGN　MR_DESIGN

うれしいを、つぎつぎと。
KIRIN

Kirin's passion combined with its brewing technology brings you the masterpiece of Happo-shu. A refreshing taste you will never forget. Enjoy it on any occasion.

GOKUNAMA
優生

www.gokunama.com キリンビール株式会社 飲酒は20歳になってから。お酒は楽しく、ほどほどに。 極生 発泡酒

極生
GOKUNAMA
Kirin's passion combined with its brewing technology brings you the masterpiece of Happo-shu. A refreshing taste you will never forget. Enjoy it on any occasion.
〈生〉
発泡酒

極生
GOKUNAMA
Kirin's passion combined with its brewing technology brings you the masterpiece of Happo-shu. A refreshing taste you will never forget. Enjoy it on any occasion.
ALC. 5.5%〈生〉
発泡酒

商品案内ポスター、パッケージ/
PRODUCT PROMOTION POSTER, PACKAGE

麒麟麦酒［酒類製造・販売］
Kirin Brewery Company,Limited ［Sales & production of alcohol beverages］
CD, AD: 佐藤可士和　Kashiwa Sato
CD: 前田知巳　Tomomi Maeda
D: 佐野研二郎　Kenjiro Sano
AGENCY & PLANNING: 博報堂　HAKUHODO Inc. /
　　　　　　　　　　　　フューチャーテクスト　FUTURE TEXT
AGENCY & PLANNING, SB: サムライ　SAMURAI Inc.

募集要項ポスター、パンフレット /
APPLICATION POSTER, BROCHURE

ガーディアンガーデン ［ギャラリー］
Guardian Garden ［Gallery］
AD, D, SB: 長嶋りかこ　Rikako Nagashima
D: 水溜友絵　Tomoe Mizutamari
DF: シロップ　Syrup

3.3 m²
PHOTOGRAPH
30TH HITOTSUBOTEN
2008.2.18(MON)〜3.6(THU)

3.3 m²
30TH HITOTSUBOTEN
ENTRY DEADLINE:
PHOTOGRAPH 2007.12.04(TUE)〜16:00
GRAPHIC ART 2008.01.15(TUE)〜20:00
一坪展

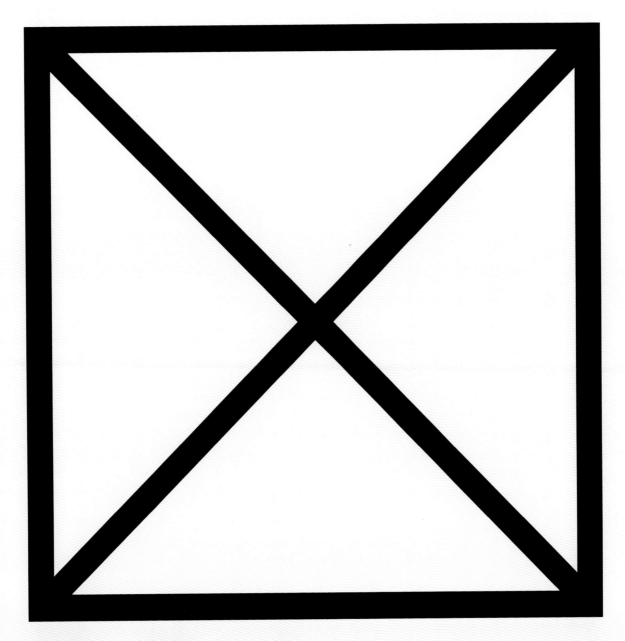

3.3 m²
30TH HITOTSUBOTEN

ENTRY DEADLINE:
PHOTOGRAPH 2007.12.04 (TUE)-20:00
GRAPHIC ART 2008.01.15 (TUE)-20:00

ABAHOUSE
LASTWORD

シーズンポスター、ノベルティ（バンダナ）/
SEASONAL POSTER, NOVELTY (BAN・DAN・NA)

アバハウスインターナショナル ［アパレル］
ABAHOUSE INTERNATIONAL CO. [Apparel]
AD, D: 野尻大作　Daisaku Nojiri
DF, SB: ground　ground

abahouse　00555

ABAHOUSE

雑誌（扉ページ）/ MAGAZINE (TITLE PAGE)

INFAS パブリケーションズ ［出版］
INFAS PUBLICATIONS,INC. ［Publisher］
D, SB: マグ　Mag

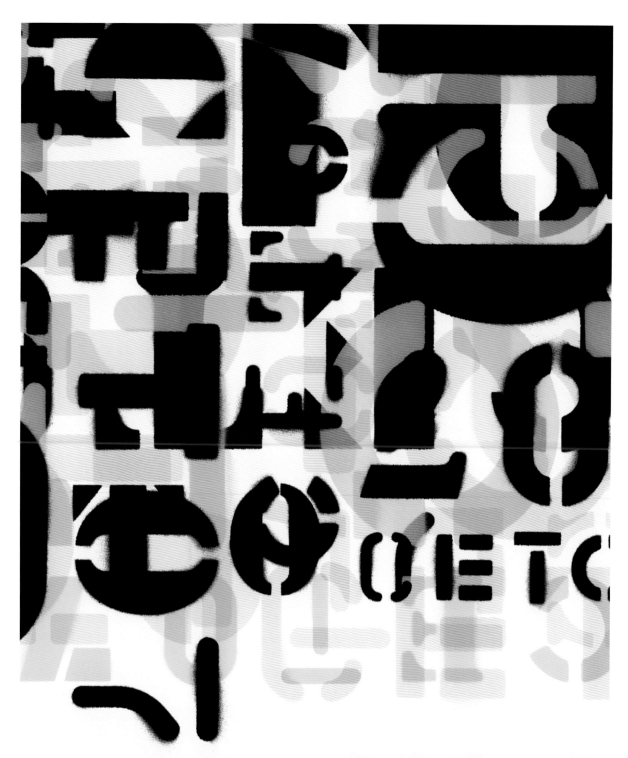

CET07
CENTRAL EAST TOKYO 2007
NIGHT×GALLERY×STREET
2007.11.23 FRI – 12.02 SUN

イベント告知ポスター /
EVENT ANNOUNCEMENT POSTER

セントラルイースト東京　[団体]
Central East Tokyo　[Association]
AD, D: 佐藤直樹　Naoki Sato / 一尾成臣　Naruomi Ichio
SB: アジール　ASYL

キミがいないと、さびしいもん。

SAPPORO ART DIRECTORS CLUB
CREATORS MEETING 2007
2007 ANNUAL PRESENTATION PARTY

DATE 2007.5.11.FRi
OPEN 18:00 / START 18:30
PLACE KING XMHU [57WN CHUOKU SAPPORO]

DESIGNED BY RYO UEDA [COMMUNE GRAPHICS]

**アワード応募要項、イベント案内状 /
AWARD GUIDELINES FOR APPLICANTS,
EVENT INVITATION**

札幌アートディレクターズクラブ ［デザイナー協会］
SAPPORO ART DIRECTORS CLUB ［Designers Organization］
AD, D, SB: 上田 亮 Ryo Ueda
DF: コミューングラフィックス COMMUNE GRAPHICS

ショップバッグ、タグ / SHOP BAG, TAG

ソスウ インターナショナル [アパレル]
SOSU international Co.,Ltd. [Apparel]
D: 三原康裕 (タグ) Yasuhiro Mihara (tag) /
WAKE UP (ショップバッグ) WAKE UP (shop bag)
SB: ソスウ インターナショナル SOSU international Co.,Ltd.

ノベルティ(チョコレート) / NOVELTY (CHOCOLATE)

アバハウスインターナショナル [アパレル]
ABAHOUSE INTERNATIONAL CO. [Apparel]
AD, D: 野尻大作 Daisaku Nojiri
P: 樋口兼一 Kenichi Higuchi
DF, SB: ground ground

コレクション案内状 / COLLECTION DM

モーテル [アパレル]
MOTEL [Apparel]
CD, AD: NESCO NESCO
D, P: 尾崎強志 (OZAKI TSUYOSHI DESIGN)
Tsuyoshi Ozaki (OZAKI TSUYOSHI DESIGN)
DF: NIGREC DESIGN NIGREC DESIGN
SB: モーテル MOTEL

コレクション案内状 / COLLECTION DM

モーテル［アパレル］
MOTEL [Apparel]
CD, AD, D: NESCO　NESCO
P: ハービー山口　Herbie Yamaguchi
DF: NIGREC DESIGN　NIGREC DESIGN
SB: モーテル　MOTEL

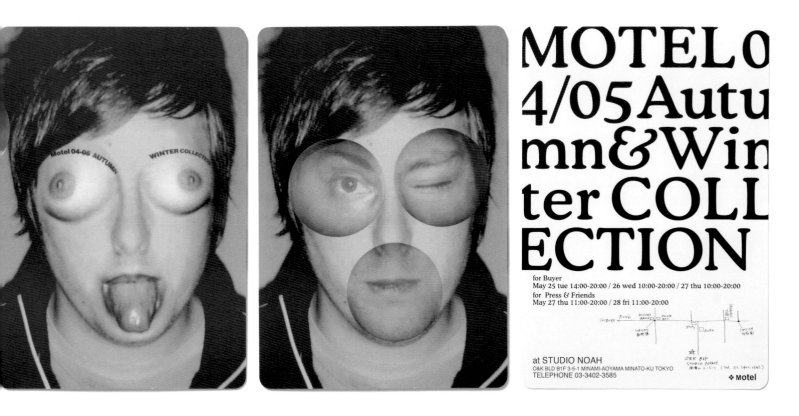

MOTEL 0
4/05 Autu
mn&Win
ter COLL
ECTION

for Buyer
May 25 tue 14:00-20:00 / 26 wed 10:00-20:00 / 27 thu 10:00-20:00
for Press & Friends
May 27 thu 11:00-20:00 / 28 fri 11:00-20:00

at STUDIO NOAH
O&K BLD B1F 3-5-1 MINAMI-AOYAMA MINATO-KU TOKYO
TELEPHONE 03-3402-3585
❖ motel

professionele muzikanten /
alle richtingen / experimenteren /
improviseren / zoeken naar
raakvlakken tussen pop-jazz-niet
westers componeerd-techno

1 dag repeteren —— 1 optreden

GASLAB, TU EINDHOVEN
WO. 27 NOVEMBER 2002
AANVANG 20.30 UUR
TOEGANG GRATIS

Arnold de Boer / **gitaar, stem**
Maxim Schram / **computer**
Nick Sanders / **bas**
Flin van Hemmen / **drums**
Broky B / **draaitafels**

Gaslab
Universiteitscampus TU/E
Den Dolech 2, Eindhoven
T 040-2472070 www.tue.nl/sg

ML B
MUZIEKLAB BRABANT Postbus 184 5000 AD Tilburg T 013 5455401 info@muzieklab.com www.muzieklab.com

MUZIEK UIT HET LAB
DI. 8 APRIL 2003
MUZIEKCENTRUM
'S-HERTOGENBOSCH
AANVANG 20.30 UUR
TOEGANG GRATIS

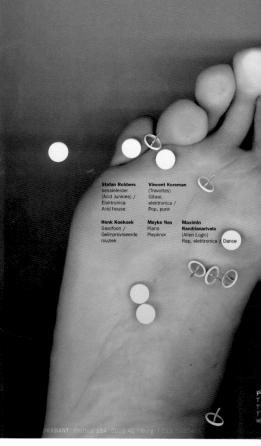

MUZIEK UIT HET LAB
DON. 13 MAART '03
PARADOX, TILBURG
AANVANG 21.30 UUR
TOEGANG GRATIS

Stefan Robbers
sessieleider
(Acid Junkies) /
Elektronica
Acid house

Vincent Koreman
(Travoltas)
Gitaar,
elektronica /
Pop, punk

Henk Koekoek
Saxofoon /
Geïmproviseerde
muziek

Mayke Nas
Piano
Piepknor

Maximin
Randrianarivelo
(Alien Logic)
Rap, elektronica / Dance

イベント告知ポスター /
EVENT ANNOUNCEMENT POSTER

MUZIEKLAB BRABANT ［劇団］
MUZIEKLAB BRABANT [Theater]
D, SB: Hans Gremmen

MUZIEK UIT HET LAB
DI. 6 MEI 2003
MUZIEKCENTRUM
'S-HERTOGENBOSCH
AANVANG 20.30 UUR
TOEGANG GRATIS

professionele muzikanten /
alle richtingen / experimenteren /
improviseren / zoeken naar
raakvlakken tussen pop-jazz-niet
westers componeerd-techno

1 dag repeteren —— 1 optreden

Jörg Lehnardt / (Sessieleider)
Elektrisch gitaar en effects
Inga Lühning / Zang
Richard van Kruysdijk /
Elektronische beats
Maurits Fondse / Fender
rhodes, synthesizer
Edward Capel / Saxofoon

Muziekcentrum
's-Hertogenbosch
Prins Bernhardstraat 4
's-Hertogenbosch
T 073-6122123
info@hetmuziekcentrum.net
www.hetmuziekcentrum.net

ML B
MUZIEKLAB BRABANT Postbus 184 5000 AD Tilburg T 013 5455401 info@muzieklab.com www.muzieklab.com

MUZIEK UIT HET LAB
professionele muzikanten / alle
richtingen / experimenteren /
improviseren / zoeken naar raakvlakken
tussen pop-jazz-niet westers
gecomponeerd-techno
1 dag repeteren: 1 optreden

Do. 16 januari 2003
Paradox, Tilburg
Aanvang 21.30 uur
Toegang gratis

Crip Theeuwes / Gitaar
Eric Maas / Bas
Joost Mantel / Vocals,
Electronica
T-mo de Kok / Drum,
Percussie
Derk van Sohie /
Toetsen, Zang

Paradox
Telegraafstraat 62, Tilburg
T 013-5432266
www.paradoxtilburg.nl

ML B
MUZIEKLAB BRABANT Postbus 184 5000 AD Tilburg T 013 5455401 info@muzieklab.com www.muzieklab.com

MUZIEK UIT HET LAB
DI. 11 FEB. 2003
MEZZ, BREDA
AANVANG 21.30 UUR
TOEGANG GRATIS

professionele muzikanten /
alle richtingen / experimenteren /
improviseren / zoeken naar
raakvlakken tussen pop-jazz-niet
westers componeerd-techno

1 dag repeteren —— 1 optreden

Lauran van der Sanden
sessieleider
klarinet, tarogato
Hedendaagse muziek

Johnny van de Koolwijk /
elektronica
Experimenteel techno

Jostijn Ligtvoet /
cello
Hedendaagse muziek

Etienne Reijnders /
mrzbuilt, elektrisch gitaar, toetsen
Metal

ML B
MUZIEKLAB BRABANT Postbus 184 5000 AD Tilburg T 013 5455401 info@muzieklab.com www.muzieklab.com

MUZIEK UIT HET LAB
Dinsdag 3 december 2002
Muziekcentrum 's-Hertogenbosch
Aanvang 20.30 uur Toegang gratis

professionele muzikanten /
alle richtingen / experimenteren /
improviseren / zoeken naar
raakvlakken tussen pop-jazz-niet
westers componeerd-techno

1 dag repeteren —— 1 optreden

Muziekcentrum 's-Hertogenbosch Prins Bernhardstraat 4 's-Hertogenbosch T 073-6122123 info@hetmuziekcentrum.net www.hetmuziekcentrum.net

| Niels Duffhues | Nick Sanders | Harmen Fraanje | Jasper le Clercq | Marko Ciciliani |
| Gitaar, Zang | Bas | Piano | Viool, Altviool | No input mixer |

Gitaar
Gitaar
Bitaar
Bitaar
Bitaar
Bitaar
Bitaar

ML B
MUZIEKLAB BRABANT Postbus 184 5000 AD Tilburg T 013 5455401 info@muzieklab.com www.muzieklab.com

展覧会告知ポスター ／
EXHIBITION ANNOUNCEMENT POSTER

5TH BERLIN BIEENIAL FOR CONTEMPORARY ART,
BERLIN, GERMANY ［団体］
5th berlin bieenial for contemporary art, Berlin, Germany ［association］
D, SB: Ludovic Balland

RAYMOND LOEWY FOUNDATION ［財団］
RAYMOND LOEWY FOUNDATION ［Foundation］
DF, SB: Heine / Lenz / Zizka

ST. MORITZ
DESIGN SUMMIT
&
INTERNATIONAL
DESIGN
ACTION DAY

RAYMOND LOEWY
FOUNDATION
INTERNATIONAL

VERLAG
DER BUCHHANDLUNG
WALTHER KÖNIG

HOW! TO TURN YOUR MONEY INTO CREATIVITY

HOW! TO TURN YOUR CREATIVITY INTO MONEY

At such times, the shape of nature's insects always seems to pass through my mind, and among them I have always thought that the design of "mizu-sumashi" (Gyrinus japonicus, whirling beetle) is brilliant. It is because all living things in nature live without waste, their shapes are indeed good teachers when it comes to design.
Kenji Ekuan

Amsterdam Tokyo

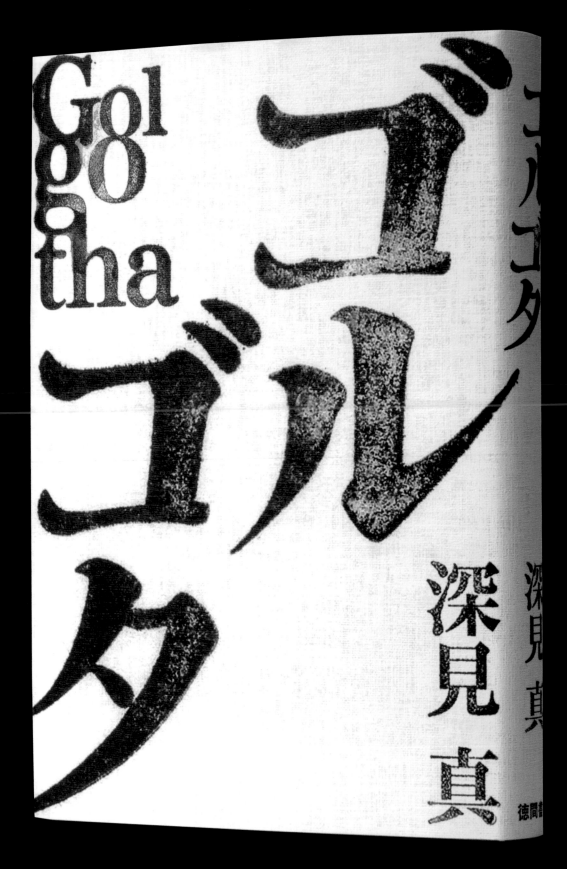

書籍／BOOK

徳間書店 ［出版］
TOKUMA SHOTEN ［Publisher］
CD: 徳間書店　TOKUMA SHOTEN
AD: 印南貴行　Takayuki Innami
D: 水澤充　Mitsuru Mizusawa
DF, SB: トーマン　THOMAIN CO.,LTD.

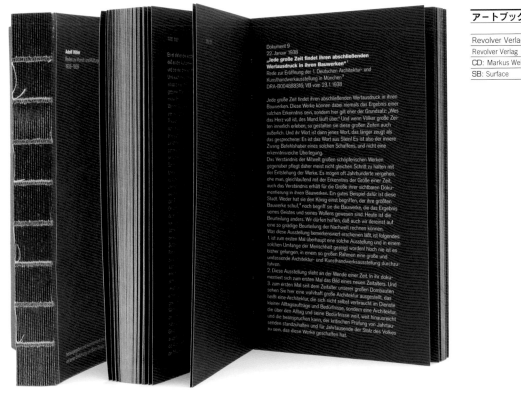

アートブック / ART BOOK

Revolver Verlag [出版社]
Revolver Verlag [Publisher]
CD: Markus Weisbeck
SB: Surface

紙見本 / PAPER SAMPLE

Antalis Hong Kong Ltd. [紙卸商社]
Antalis Hong Kong Ltd. [Paper Company]
AD: Eddy Yu / Hung Lam
D: Luke Lo
SB: Co Design Ltd.

CD

ランブリング・レコーズ [レコードレーベル]
Rambling Records [Record label]
AD, D: 井上広一 Koichi Inoue
DF, SB: オーイェル ORYEL

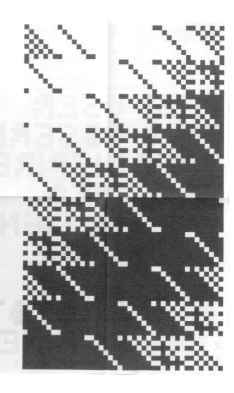

展覧会告知ポスター／
EXHIBITION ANNOUNCEMENT POSTER

SIX CITIES DESIGN FESTIVAL ［展覧会］
Six Cities Design Festival ［Exhibition］
D: Hector Pottie
SB: Third Eye Design

書籍／BOOK

アンドーギャラリー［アート・建築・デザインのプロデュース］
ANDO GALLERY,INC. [Art, architecture, design produce]
AD: 北川一成　Issay Kitagawa
D: 杉江由夏　Yuka Sugie
DF, SB: グラフ　GRAPH CO.,LTD.

INDEX

SUBMITTORS

JAPAN

あ

アートレス
artless Inc. 031, 142

アヴェダ
Aveda Coroporation 138

アサツー・ディ・ケイ
ASATSU-DK INC. 096, 097

アジール
ASYL 182

アンテナグラフィックベース
ANTENNA GRAPHIC BASE CO.,LTD. 141

イー
E.Co.,Ltd. 024, 025, 026, 150, 163

イヤマデザイン
iyamadesign 061

氏デザイン
ujidesign 102

Hd Lab
Hd Lab Inc. 044, 045, 124

エスジー
SG 175

エヌ・ジー
N.G.INC., 040, 041, 058, 059, 130, 131, 176

オーイェル
ORYEL 191

か

グッドデザインカンパニー
good design company 017, 030, 060, 088, 095, 151, 162, 163

GROUND
ground 029, 036, 037, 042, 043, 068, 069, 104, 105, 106, 107, 136, 137, 159, 180, 181, 184

グラフ
GRAPH CO.,LTD. 108, 192

グラフレックスディレクションズ
Graflex Directions 101, 108

グランツ
Glanz 144, 145

クリ・ラボ
KURI-LAB. 016, 125

グリッツデザイン
gritzdesign inc. 046, 047, 100, 116, 117, 118, 119, 160

グルービジョンズ
groovisions 086, 087, 103

小杉幸一
KOICHI KOSUGI 089, 172

コミューングラフィックス
COMMUNE GRAPHICS 035, 048, 049, 089, 183

さ

サムライ
SAMURAI Inc, 076, 077, 078, 079, 122, 123, 178

資生堂
Shiseido CO.,LTD. 062, 074, 075, 141

スタジオ
STUDIO 090

スリーアンドコー
Three&co, 028, 039

スロウ
SLOW inc. 027

ソスウ インターナショナル
SOSU international Co.,Ltd. 135, 184

た

ダイナマイト・ブラザーズ・シンジケート
Dynamite Brothers Syndicate 132, 133

タグボートツー
TUGBOAT2 072, 073

デイリー・フレッシュ
Dairy Fresh 052

デキスギ
DEKISUGI 094

電通
DENTSU INC. 056, 057

トーマン
THOMAN CO.,LTD. 190

ドッポ
doppo inc.   120, 121
ドラフト
DRAFT Co.,Ltd.   018, 019, 020, 021, 022, 023,
                           110, 111, 112, 113, 114, 115
トンプー・グラフィクス
tong-poo graphics   161

な
長嶋りかこ
Rikako Nagashima   066, 067, 070, 071, 073, 178, 179
仲條デザイン事務所
Nakajo Design Office   169
西岡ペンシル
Nishioka Pencil Co.,Ltd.   054, 055
日本デザインセンター
NIPPON DESIGN CENTER,INC.   010, 011

は
博報堂
HAKUHODO Inc.   013, 014, 015, 050, 051, 053, 095, 173, 177
バタフライストローク
butterfly stroke inc,   103, 140, 141
パブリックデザインワークス
PUBLIC DESIGN WORKS INC.   061
浜田武士
Takeshi Hamada   030
HISAZUMI DESIGN
Hisazumi design Inc,   128, 129
ビームスクリエイティブ
BEAMS CREATIVE Inc,   123
プラグイングラフィック
PLUG-IN GRAPHIC   146, 154, 155, 158, 159, 164, 165

ま
マグ
Mag   181

MR_DESIGN
MR_DESIGN   013, 050, 051, 053, 095, 168, 173, 177
モーデザイン
mo'design inc   082, 083
モーテル
MOTEL   084, 085, 134, 135, 142, 156, 184, 185

や
ユニクロ
UNIQLO CO.,LTD.   038
米津智之
Tomoyuki Yonezu   012, 171

わ
ワイデン+ケネディ トウキョウ
Wieden+Kennedy Tokyo   032, 033, 034, 035, 098, 099

OVERSEAS

Alexander Gelman   147
CoDesign Ltd.   092, 093, 191
DNS-Transport GmbH   152
Erich Brechbuhl   174
FK DESIGN SRL   139
Form   137, 157
Hans Gremmen   167, 186, 187
Heine / Lenz / Zizka   189
homework   064, 065
Karin van Dam   127
Kessels Kramer   91
KIOSK   153
Ludovic Balland   188
M/M [PARIS]   148, 149
Scandinavian DesignLab   126
Surface   191
Third Eye Design   192
WORK   080, 081, 096, 097, 166

IN-STORE DISPLAY GRAPHICS

店頭コミュニケーショングラフィックス

Page: 216 (Full Color)　¥14,000+Tax

店頭でのプロモーション展開においては、空間デザインだけでなくグラフィックデザインが果たす役割も重要です。本書では、空間のイメージとグラフィックツールのコンセプトが一貫している作品をはじめ、限られたスペースで有効活用できるディスプレーキットや、P.O.P. の役割も果たすショップツールなどを広く紹介します。

A useful display tool for a limited space, display examples which show the harmonization among packaging, shop interior and in-store promotional graphics, a creative point-of-sale tool which stands out among others. This book is a perfect resource for designers and marketing professionals.

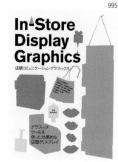
995

CHARACTER DESIGN TODAY

キャラクターデザイン・トゥデイ

Page: 232 (Full Color)　¥14,000+Tax

キャラクターは企業と消費者とを結ぶ有効なコミュニケーションツールといえます。競合商品との差別化をはかるため、企業のサービスを消費者にわかりやすく伝えるためなど、その役割は様々です。本書では、キャラクターのデザインコンセプト、プロフィールとともに広告やツールの展開例を収録。巻頭では、キャラクターが決定するまでの過程やボツ案を特集し、長く愛されるキャラクターをデザインするポイントを探ります。

200 successful characters with each profile, concept as well as the graphic examples. A featured article about the process of creating a character from scratch is also included with useful examples.

984

NEO JAPANESQUE GRAPHICS

ネオ ジャパネスクグラフィックス

Page: 208 (Full Color)　¥14,000+Tax

近年、さまざまなデザイン作品のなかに、伝統的な和風意匠から脱却し、より現代的に洗練され、アレンジされた新しい和テイストのデザインが数多く見られるようになりました。本書は、広告・装幀・パッケージなどのカテゴリごとに、各分野の優れた"新・和風デザイン"を紹介します。次世代の和風デザインが集結した見ごたえのある1冊として、あらゆるクリエイターにお薦めします。

This collection presents a tremendous array of the next generation Japanese-style design that is currently drawn attention in creative circles as expressed in the form of flyers, catalogs, posters, packaging, CD jackets, calendars, book design, and more.

858

PACKAGE FORM AND DESIGN

ペーパーパッケージデザイン大全集　作例＆展開図(CD-ROM付)

Page: 240 (Full Color)　¥7,800+Tax

大好評の折り方シリーズ第3弾。製品を守りブランドアイデンティティーのアピールとなるパッケージ。本書ではバラエティーに富んだかたちのペーパーパッケージ約200点を国内外から集め、その作例と展開図を紹介していきます。展開図を掲載したCD-ROM付きでクリエイターやパッケージ制作に関わる人たちの参考資料として永久保存版の1冊です。

This is the third title focusing on paper packaging in "Encyclopedia of Paper Folding Design" series. The 150 high quality works are all created by the industry professionals; the perfect shapes and beautiful designs are practical and yet artistic. The template files in pdf file on CD-ROM.

941

GIRLY GRAPHICS

ガーリー グラフィックス

Page: 200 (Full Color)　¥9,800+Tax

"ガーリー"とは女の子らしさの見直しや、ポップでありながらもキュートといった、女の子らしさを楽しむポジティブな姿勢を意味します。そんな"ガーリー"な空気感を、ポスター・DM・カタログ・パッケージなどのデザイン領域で、魅力的に表現した作品を紹介します。

A word "girly" represents an expression of reconstructing positive images about being girls. Today, those powerful and contagious "girly" images with great impact successfully grab attentions not only from girls but also from a broad range of audience. This book features about those 300 enchanted and fascinated advertisements such as posters, catalogs, shop cards, business cards, books, CD jackets, greeting cards, letterheads, product packages and more.

1009

NEO JAPANESQUE DESIGN

ネオ ジャパネスク デザイン

Page: 224 (Full Color)　¥14,000+Tax

2006年2月に発刊し好評を得た「ネオ ジャパネスク グラフィックス」。待望の第二弾「ネオ ジャパネスク デザイン」がいよいよ登場。ショップイメージ・ロゴ＆マークのカテゴリが新たに加わり、内容・クオリティともにバージョンアップした"和"デザインの最前線を紹介します。

This is the sister edition to "Neo Japanesque Graphics" published in 2006, and this new book includes even more modern yet Japanese taste designs which will give creative professionals inspirational ideas for their projects. Among various graphic works, this second title features shop design such as restaurants, bars and hotels, also features a variety of Japanese logos.

996

文字を読ませる広告デザイン 2

Page: 192 (Full Color)　¥9,800+Tax

パッと見た時に文字が目に入ってきて、しかも読みやすいデザインの広告物やパッケージの特集です。優れたデザインや文字組み、コピーによって見る側に文字・文章を読ませることを第一に考えられた広告を厳選します。ポスター、新聞広告、チラシ、車内吊り、雑誌広告、DM、カタログ、パンフレット、本の装丁、パッケージ、看板・サインなど多岐なジャンルにわたり紹介します。

Sales in Japan only.

934

NEW ENCYCLOPEDIA OF PAPER-FOLDING DESIGNS

折り方大全集　カタログ・DM編（CD-ROM付）

Page: 240 (160 in Color)　¥7,800+Tax

デザインの表現方法の1つとして使われている『折り』。日頃何気なく目にしているDMやカード、企業のプロモーション用カタログなど身近なデザイン中に表現されている『折り』から、たたむ機能やせり出す、たわめる機能まで、約200点の作品を展開図で示し、『折り』を効果的に生かした実際の作品を掲載しています。

More than 200 examples of direct mail, cards, and other familiar printed materials featuring simple / multiple folds, folding up, and insertion shown as they are effected by folding along with flat diagrams of their prefolded forms. With CD-ROM.

490

DESIGN IDEAS FOR RENEWAL

再生グラフィックス

Page: 240 (Full Color)　¥14,000+Tax

本書では "再生" をキーワードにデザインの力で既存の商業地や施設、ブランドを甦らせた事例を特集します。リニューアル後のグラフィックツールを中心に、デザインコンセプトや再生後の効果についても紹介します。企業や地域の魅力を再活性させるためにデザインが果たした役割を実感できる1冊です。

A collection of case studies - with "regeneration" and "renewal" as their keywords - showing commercial districts, facilities and brands brought back to life through the power of design. Focusing on mainly the post-renovation graphic tools, we present the design concepts and their regenerative effects through which readers will see the role that design can play in reigniting the allure of companies and communities.

977

GRAPHIC SIMPLICITY

シンプル グラフィックス

Page: 248 (Full Color)　¥14,000+Tax

上質でシンプルなデザイン——見た目がすっきりとして美しいのはもちろんのこと、シンプルなのに個性的な作品、カラフルなのに上品な作品、フォントやロゴがさりげなく効いている作品など、その洗練されたデザインは見る人を魅了してやみません。本書は厳選された作品を国内外から集め、落ち着いた大人の雰囲気にまとめ上げた本物志向のグラフィックコレクションです。

Simple, high-quality design work: not just crisply elegant and eye catching, but uncluttered yet distinctive, colorful yet refined, making subtly effective use of fonts and logos; in short, sophisticated design that seduces all who sees it.

973

1&2 COLOR EDITORIAL DESIGN

１・２色でみせるエディトリアルデザイン

Page: 160 (Full Color)　¥7,800+Tax

少ない色数でエディトリアルデザインする際には、写真の表現や本文使用色に制限がある分、レイアウトや使用する紙に工夫や表現力が問われます。本書は1色、2色で魅力的にレイアウトされた作品を、インクや用紙データのスペックと併せて紹介します。

This book presents many of well-selected editorial design examples, featuring unique and outstanding works using one or two colors. All works in this single volume present designers enormous hints for effective and unique techniques with information on specs of inks and papers. Examples include PR pamphlets, magazines, catalogs, company brochures, and books.

956

PICTGRAM & ICON GRAPHICS 2

ピクトグラム＆アイコングラフィックス 2

Page: 208 (Full Color)　¥13,000+Tax

本書では、視覚化に成功した国内・海外のピクトグラムとアイコンを紹介します。空港・鉄道・病院・デパート・動物園といった施設の案内サインとして使用されているピクトグラムやマップ・フロアガイドをはじめ、雑誌やカタログの中で使用されているアイコンなど、身近なグラフィックまでを業種別に掲載。巻末に、一般的によく使われるピクトグラム（トイレ・エスカレーター・駐車場など）の種類別一覧表を収録。

Second volume of the best-seller title "Pictogram and Icon Graphics". Full-loaded with the latest pictograms around the world. Signage, floor guides and maps in airport, railway, hospital, department store, zoo and many more. Contained a wide variety of icons, including those found in catalogs and magazines, etc.

935

FASHION BRAND GRAPHICS

ファッション グラフィックス

Page: 160 (Full Color)　¥7,800+Tax

本書は、ファッション、アパレルにおけるグラフィックデザインに力を入れた販促ツールを、厳選して紹介します。通常のショップツールはもちろん、シーズンごと、キャンペーンごとのツールも掲載。激しく移り変わるファッション業界において、お客様を飽きさせない、華やかで魅力的な作品を凝縮した1冊です。

The fashion brands that appear in this collection are among the most highly regarded in Japan and herein we introduce some of their commonly used marketing tools including catalogues, shopping cards and shopping bags, together with their seasonal promotional tools and novelties. This publication serves for not only graphic designers, but also people in the fashion industry, marketing professionals.

962

BEST FLYER 365DAYS NEWSPAPER INSERT EDITION

ベストチラシ 365 デイズ　折込チラシ編

Page: 256 (Full Color)　¥14,000+Tax

一番身近な広告媒体である新聞の折込チラシ。地域に密着したお得な情報を提供するものから、セレブ&クールで夢のようなビジュアルのものまで多種多様です。本書では、1年間（365日）の各セールスシーズンでまとめたものから、1枚だけで効果的に商品をPRしたチラシまで、優れたデザインの旬な折込チラシ800点を収録しています。広告の制作に携わる人びとに必携のデザインサンプル集です。

This book contains many examples of excellently designed, topical flyers, ranging from seasonal advertisements to flyers for a single product. It is an anthology of design samples for creative professionals in the advertising industry.

936

BEYOND ADVERTISING: COMMUNICATION DESIGN

コミュニケーション デザイン

Page: 224 (Full Color)　¥15,000+Tax

限られた予算のなか、ターゲットへ確実に届く、費用対効果の高い広告をどのように実現するか？ 今デザイナーには、広告デザインだけでなく、コミュニケーション方法までもデザインすることが求められています。本書では「消費者との新しいコミュニケーションのカタチ」をテーマに実施されたキャンペーンの事例を幅広く紹介。様々なキャンペーンを通して、コミュニケーションを成功させるヒントを探求します。

Reaching the target market a limited budget: how is cost effective promotion achieved? What are the most effective ways to combine print and digital media? What expression reaches the target market? The answers lie in this book, with "new ways and forms of communicating with the consumer" as its concept.

948

WORLD CALENDAR DESIGN

ワールドカレンダーデザイン

Page: 224 (Full Color)　¥9,800+Tax

本書では国内外のクリエーターから集めたカレンダーを特集します。優れたグラフィックスが楽しめるスタンダードなタイプから、形状のユニークなもの、仕掛けのあるものなど、形状別にカテゴリーに分けて紹介します。カレンダー制作のデザインソースとしてはもちろん、ユニークな作品を通して、様々なグラフィックスに活かせるアイデアが実感できる内容です。

The newest and most distinctive calendars from designers around the world. The collection features a variety of calendar types highly selected from numerous outstanding works ranging from standard wall calendars to unique pieces in form and design, including lift-the flap calendar, 3D calendar, pencil calendar and more.

949

GRAPHIC TOOLS IN SERVICE BUSINESSES
サービス業の案内グラフィックス

Page: 224 (Full Color)　¥14,000＋Tax

ハードウェアからソフトウェアへの移行にともなう通信関連業、既に定着した働く女性増加における代行業、高齢化社会における介護・医療業務など、社会は今、サービス業の需要が確実に増え、生活に欠かせないものとなっています。本書ではサービス内容を案内するカタログ・リーフレットを中心に、その他広告ツールも併せて紹介します。

930

The demands for service industries have become an indispensable part of life in the world today. This book looks at the sucessful campaigns of competitive service businesses ranging from telecommunications, internet, finance to restaurants, hotels and clinics. This is a good resource not only for designers but marketing professionals.

CORPORATE PROFILE & IMAGE
業種別 企業案内グラフィックス

Page: 256 (Full Color)　¥15,000＋Tax

本書は会社案内を中心に、学生が求める情報と使いやすさを熟慮した入社案内や、その企業の持つ個性を凝縮したコンセプトブック、会社のイメージアップにつながる企業広告などをさまざまな業種にわたり収録。単なる会社のスペック案内だけにとどまらない、企業理念やメッセージを社内外にわかりやすく的確に伝える、デザイン性に優れた作品を紹介します。

877

A collection of print materials that help create and support corporate image in a wide range of industries: company profiles as well as concept books designed to epitomize company character, corporate ads designed specially to improve company image, recruiting brochures, and more.

LOCAL BRAND DESIGN
地域ブランド戦略のデザイン

Pages: 224 (Full Color)　¥14,000＋Tax

地域特性を活かした商品・サービスのブランド化と地域イメージのブランド化を結びつけ、全国レベルのブランド展開を目指す「地域ブランド戦略」の取り組みが全国各地で積極的に行われています。本書ではデザイナーが地域ブランド戦略に関わることで認知度アップに成功した実例を紹介します。地方自治体のキャンペーン展開や目を引く特産品のパッケージ、ショップのグラフィックツールなどのアイテムを多数収録。

917

This title features the brand marketing strategies for products and services available only in the limited area in Japan. Each brand is created based on the unique identity for the local area, which draws peopleÅfs attention and leads to nationwide the brand recognition.

SALES STRATEGY AND DESIGN
販売戦略とデザイン

Page: 224 (Full Color)　¥15,000＋Tax

様々な業種の商品発売（サービス業の商品も含む）に伴う告知プロモーションを商品ごとに紹介。思わず手に取るネーミングや、店頭で目を引くパッケージ、消費者の心をくすぐるノベルティなど、各々のアイテムを巧みに利用した例を多数収録。

Unique and outstanding graphic tools in new product/service launching. Here are packages, novelties and the naming of product offering the newest communication styles to consumers!! With explanation of concept and motive for product / promotional tools.

790

販売戦略と
デザイン
は、切っても切れ
ない関係というの
が、この本のあら
すじです。

Sales Strategy and Design

NEW SHOP IMAGE GRAPHICS 2
ニュー ショップイメージ グラフィックス 2

Page: 224 (Full Color)　¥15,000＋Tax

お店の個性を強く打ち出すためには、販売戦略と明確なコンセプトに基づいた、ショップのイメージ作りが重要です。本書は様々な業種からデザイン性の高いショップアイデンティティ展開を、グラフィックツールと店舗写真、コンセプト文を交え紹介。

789

Second volume of the best seller titls in overseas. New Shop Image Graphics released in 2002. This book covers the latest, unique and impressive graphics in interiors and exteriors of various shops as well as their supporting materials.

SHOP IMAGE GRAPHICS IN LONDON
ショップイメージ グラフィックスイン ロンドン

Pages: 192 (Full Color)　¥9,800＋Tax

コンラン卿に影響を受けたモダンテイストのインテリアショップやデザインホテル、ユースカルチャーの中心的存在である音楽やアパレルショップ、ナチュラル志向のオーガニックレストランやスパ、エステなどロンドンならではの個性的なショップを厳選して紹介します。モダンな最新ショップからクラシカルな老舗店まで、今最もエキサイティングな都市ロンドンのショップアイデンティティ特集です。

933

Features 97 London shops and shows the intimate connection between the city's history and the street design, which's influenced internationally. The presented examples are dominated by these broad designs: classic, modern, and exotic.

ABSOLUTE APPEAL: DIRECT MAIL DESIGN
魅せる掴むDMデザイン

Page: 224 (Full Color)　¥14,000＋Tax

ターゲットをつかむために様々な工夫が凝らされたDMを厳選し、その制作意図にまで踏み込んで紹介します。素材や形状など、取り上げたDMのポイントとなる部分をレイアウトで大胆に見せていくほか、デザインの狙いを文字情報で提供し、表現に込められた"戦略"を分かりやすくひも解きます。

925

This book introduces a variety of DM that have succeeded in captivating the target audience and winning their hearts. Many of the photos focus on the quality of the materials in an effort to provide the reader with a sense of what is the most distinguishing feature of DM, something that is normally gained only by picking them up and feeling them.

書き文字・装飾文字 グラフィックス

Page: 192 (Full Color)　¥9,800＋Tax

普段使われるフォントではなく、手書きや装飾された個性的な文字を使用したグラフィック作品を紹介。筆文字は力強く和のイメージを、ペン文字はラフでやさしいイメージを感じさせます。文字選びは作品のイメージを左右する重要なポイントです。

Sales in Japan only.

787

FOOD PACKAGE DESIGN

フードパッケージ デザイン

Page: 160 (Full Color)　¥7,800+Tax

ところ狭しと並んだ食品の棚で、いかに目を引き美味しそうにみえるか、インパクトと洗練されたデザインが求められるのが食品パッケージ。ショップのイメージと統一された戦略的デザインや、スーパーマーケットのオリジナルパッケージ、形の面白さを追求したパッケージなど、世界中から選りすぐった、新しい発想の食品パッケージを約400点紹介します。

A collection presenting a wide variety of packaging for foods from all corners of the world. The some 400 carefully selected works shown within are distinctive for their unified marketing strategies linked to product and store image, their interesting forms and use of color, their aesthetic pursuits and more.

896

COSMETICS PACKAGE DESIGN

コスメパッケージ & ボトル デザイン

Page: 160 (Full Color)　¥7,800+Tax

化粧品、ヘルスケア用品（シャンプー・石鹸・入浴剤・整髪剤）のパッケージ、ボトルやチューブのデザインを中心に紹介。また、それらの商品しおり、ディスプレイ写真もあわせて掲載。「今、女性にウケるデザインとは？」がわかる1冊です。

Cosmetics and personal care products and their packaging represent the state of the art in design sensitive to the tastes of contemporary women. This collection presents a wide range of flowery, elegant, charming, and unique packages for makeup, skin-care, body, bath, and hair-care products and fragrances selected from all over the world.

526

FREE PAPER GRAPHICS

フリーペーパー グラフィックス

Pages: 240 (Full Color)　¥14,000+Tax

手軽な情報ツール・新しい広告媒体として注目される今話題のフリーペーパー。専門誌並みに詳しい内容のものから、ファッションやカルチャーなど市販雑誌に負けない充実した内容のものまで多種多様。本書ではデザイン性の高い、優れたフリーペーパーを厳選し、総合情報・地域情報・専門情報の3つに分類して紹介しています。巻末には各誌の年間 "特集タイトル" を掲載。この1冊でフリーペーパーの "今" がわかります。

Free papers are fast becoming the talk of the industry as a new advertising medium and a more casual, inexpensive communications tool. This collection presents a carefully selected array of well-designed free papers grouped in three categories: general, regional, and specialty information.

907

EARTH-FRIENDLY GRAPHICS

ロハス グラフィックス

Page: 240 (Full Color)　¥14,000+Tax

ロハス(LOHAS - life style of Health and Sustainability)とは地球環境保護と健康な生活を最優先し、人類と地球が共存できる持続可能なライフスタイルのこと。ここ数年で日本のロハス人口は増加し、ロハスをコンセプトにした商品の売れ行きは好調です。本書では地球と人にやさしい商品のコンセプトとともに広告・販促ツール・パッケージデザインまでを業種別のコンテンツにわけて分かりやすく紹介します。

"Earth-Friendly Graphics" is a collection of unique graphic communications including package design, promotional tools and advertising for environmental-friendly products and services based on the concept of Lifestyles of Health and Sustainability (LOHAS), the focus of increasing attention in recent years.

902

GUIDE SIGN GRAPHICS

ガイドサイン グラフィックス

Page: 272 (Full color)　¥14,000+Tax

近年、さまざまな施設で見られる「ガイドサイン」。ユニバーサルを意識した病院の色彩デザインや、地方の私立大学の個性を活かしたインテリアサイン、その他、美術館や空港など、利用者の世代や使用言語が異なる人々が利用する施設にこそ、わかりやすい、優れたサインが見られます。本書は豊富な使用実例を見せながら、時代のニーズに合わせた国内と海外のサインシステムをご紹介します。

Sign systems are designed to meet the demands of the times. It's in facilities used by different ages, or speaking different languages, that the most user-friendly signage can be found. This book presents an extensive collection of photographs, examples of guide signs in practical use, and is an essential reference for designers.

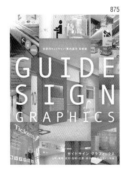

875

URBAN SIGN DESIGN

最新 看板・サイン大全集　（CD-ROM付）

Page: 256 (Full Color)　¥15,000+Tax

街を彩るさまざまな看板を飲食・製造・販売・サービスなど業種別にまとめて紹介。256ページのボリュームに加え、掲載写真の収録CD-ROMも付いた看板デザイン集の決定版。サイン業界のプロから、あらゆるクリエイターにお薦めしたい1冊です。

From among the many signs that flood city streetscapes, we've selected only the most striking, the most beautiful, the most tasteful, and present them here categorized by industry: restaurant, manufacturing, retail, and service. A whopping 256 pages of signs ranging from world-renowned brands to local restaurants, this single volume is sure to provide a source of ideas with a CD-ROM.

836

カタログ・新刊のご案内について

総合カタログ、新刊案内をご希望の方は、はさみ込みのアンケートはがきをご返送いただくか、下記ピエ・ブックスへご連絡下さい。

CATALOGS and INFORMATION ON NEW PUBLICATIONS

If you would like to receive a free copy of our general catalog or details of our new publications, please fill out the enclosed postcard and return it to us by mail or fax.

CATALOGUES ET INFORMATIONS SUR LES NOUVELLES PUBLICATIONS

Si vous désirez recevoir un exemplaire qratuit de notre catalogue généralou des détails sur nos nouvelles publication. veuillez compléter la carte réponse incluse et nous la retourner par courrierou par fax.

CATALOGE und INFORMATIONEN ÜBER NEUE TITLE

Wenn Sie unseren Gesamtkatalog oder Detailinformationen über unsere neuen Titel wünschen.fullen Sie bitte die beigefügte Postkarte aus und schicken Sie sie uns per Post oder Fax.

ピエ・ブックス

〒170-0005　東京都豊島区南大塚2-32-4
TEL: 03-5395-4811　FAX: 03-5395-4812
www.piebooks.com

PIE BOOKS

2-32-4 Minami-Otsuka Toshima-ku Tokyo 170-0005 JAPAN
TEL : +81-3-5395-4811 FAX : +81-3-5395-4812
www.piebooks.com

男グラフィックス
TOUGH-STYLE GRAPHICS

JACKET & COVER DESIGN
ART DIRECTOR / DESIGNER
野尻大作　Daisaku Nojiri

DESIGNER
高松 セリア サユリ　Célia Sayuri Takamatsu

PHOTOGRAPHER
藤本 邦治　Kuniharu Fujimoto

TRANSLATOR
パメラ ミキ　Pamela Miki

EDITORIAL ASSISTANCE
白倉美紀子　Mikiko Shirakura

EDITOR
関田理恵　Rie Sekita

PUBLISHER
三芳 伸吾　Shingo Miyoshi

2008年4月14日　初版第1刷発行

発行所　ピエ・ブックス
〒170-0005　東京都豊島区南大塚2-32-4
編集 Tel: 03-5395-4820　Fax: 03-5395-4821
e-mail: editor@piebooks.com
営業 Tel: 03-5395-4811　Fax: 03-5395-4812
e-mail: sales@piebooks.com
http://www.piebooks.com

印刷・製本　(株)サンニチ印刷